An Anc
Egyptian

An Ancient Egyptian Herbal

Lise Manniche

Published in co-operation with
BRITISH MUSEUM PRESS

UNIVERSITY OF TEXAS PRESS, AUSTIN

To J.A.R. Harris

International Standard Book Number 0-292-70415-1
Library of Congress Catalog Card Number 89-50028

Second University of Texas Press printing, 1993

Requests for permission to reproduce material
from this work should be sent to Permissions,
University of Texas Press,
Box 7819, Austin, Texas 78713-7819.

Contents

Acknowledgements

I am indebted to F. Nigel Hepper, B.Sc., F.I.Biol., of the Herbarium, Kew Gardens, for reading the manuscript and weeding out any botanical errors; to Professor J. R. Harris, School of Oriental Studies, Durham, for providing me with a list of the as yet unpublished plant material from the tomb of Tutankhamun, and to Dr J. Málek of the Griffith Institute, Oxford, for supplying additional information. I also wish to thank Mr F. Gouverneur of The Islamic Texts Society, Cambridge, for allowing me to study in typescript a translation by Dr P. Johnstone of *Al-tibb al-Nabawi* (The Medicine of the Prophet) currently in press. Dr D. M. Dixon, University College London, read the manuscript and kindly assisted with some of the photographs. Finally, to Professor G. T. Martin, University College London, I owe a number of bibliographical references as well as generous use of his library.

A sycamore tree.
Wall-painting in Theban
Tomb no. 217;
Ramesside.

Introduction

In Egypt the use of plants goes back to remote antiquity, and the tradition has survived until the present day. In the market of any town herbs and spices are for sale for culinary and medicinal purposes. In the Middle Ages, when Islamic science was at its height, the use of herbs in medicine was the subject of major treatises for which the Arabs are justly famous. They in turn had extracted their information from the learned books of their earlier Greek counterparts, to which was added the knowledge of local plants which had been used in folk medicine for centuries. The herbal tradition was kept alive by the Copts, early Christians who were direct descendants of the ancient Egyptians. The Egyptians in the days of the pharaohs had developed great skill in the use of herbs. The earliest medical texts, some four thousand years old, rely chiefly on the rich choice of plants which the land was able to produce.

No complete ancient Egyptian herbal has yet been found, but a few fragments dating from the second century AD survive. Some come from an illustrated herbal papyrus written in Greek, but found and used in Egypt. Others are part of a herbal written in a late form of the Egyptian language. It is without illustrations, but composed so as to give the name of the plant, its habitat and main characteristics, and the purpose for which it was used. These were manifold, for apart from their medicinal application, flowers, seeds and fruits, leaves, roots, bark and chips of wood found use in cosmetics and perfumery; in cookery; and in the house as ornaments or in preparations. In the present work all these parts of vegetation are often loosely referred to as 'herbs'.

The Egyptian garden

Few things are more enjoyable in a warm climate than to sit in the shade of a tree and contemplate one's garden, catching the fragrance of the flowers and listening to the sounds of the birds and insects. The ancient Egyptians were as proud of their gardens as their modern descendants, and the larger gardens, such as those belonging to the temples, must have been truly spectacular. The gardens of private individuals were occasionally depicted on the walls of their tomb chapels, and we are thus able to see with our own eyes how the Egyptians planted their trees, herbs and flowers.

There is no reason to believe that the artist's rendering of his motif differed substantially from reality: a formal garden was the aim, with trees in neat rows and flowers in square beds or straight borders. The town-dweller had little room at his disposal, but he could choose to build his residence around an existing tree, which would then be left standing in the courtyard of the house. Nebamun, a police captain of King Tuthmosis IV (*c.*1405 BC), opted for this solution in his Theban residence. A painting in his tomb shows two palm trees towering over a house built of mud-brick washed with pink. The owner of a town house, avid for greenery, would plant additional trees and shrubs in pots and other containers and place these along the façade of his house, and probably in the inside courtyard as well.

When more space was available a fishpond became the centre-piece in even a very small garden. Meketre, chancellor to King Mentuhotpe II, had models of the houses and workshops on his estate buried in a secret chamber under the floor of his tomb chapel when he died around 2000 BC. These little dolls' houses included two models of his villa and garden – in fact, the garden predominates, for the house itself is reduced to a portico. In the model the walled garden includes a fishpond surrounded by sycamore trees, delicately sculpted in wood and painted a bright green.

The town house of the police captain Nebamun. Wall-painting in his tomb at Thebes (no. 90); 18th Dynasty.

8

Among representations of private ornamental gardens one from the tomb of a scribe of the granary called Nebamun stands out (*c.* 1380 BC). In the fishpond lotus flowers float on the surface of the water, and the black fertile mud on its banks has been planted with a mixed herbaceous border. Among the trees bordering the pond is an unusually prolific mandrake. The trees include *carica* figs and sycamore figs; date-palm and *dôm*-palm; and, in the lower left-hand corner, an unsupported vine. We can only speculate about the identity of three fruitless trees. The top right-hand corner of the scene is a reminder that however idyllic and realistic the painting may seem, it does come from a tomb and is part of a larger funerary context: a female figure emerges from the tree, bearing provisions. She is Hathor or Nut, the sycamore goddess, who was included to provide for the tomb-owner in the Hereafter.

Some hundred years before Nebamun watched the efforts of his chosen tomb artist to depict his ideal garden, a builder called Ineni carried out plans on a grander scale. Ineni was in charge of the building activities of King Tuthmosis I (1528–1510 BC), and of those of his successors, but he also provided a residence

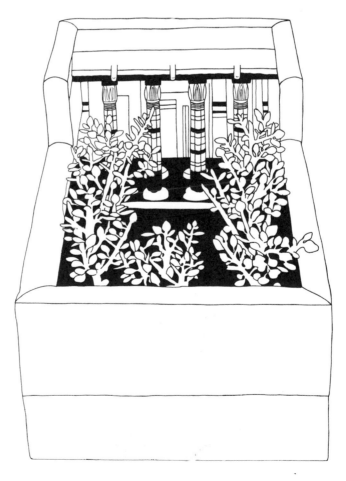

A model of the villa and garden of Meketre, chancellor to King Mentuhotpe II. From his tomb at Thebes (no. 280). Metropolitan Museum of Art, New York.

The garden of Nebamun, accountant of the granary. Wall-painting from his tomb at Thebes; 18th Dynasty. British Museum (37983).

for himself whose main attraction was a magnificent garden. A view of the house and the garden behind, with its fishpond, is depicted in Ineni's tomb, but the painter was unable to do it full justice. As he could only fit in a selection of the trees, arranged in neat rows, Ineni made sure that a complete inventory of the trees he planted in his orchard was included: 73 sycamore trees; 31 persea trees; 170 date-palms; 120 *dôm*-palms; 5 fig trees; 2 moringa trees; 12 vines; 5 pomegranate trees; 16 carob trees; 5 Christ thorn; 1 *argûn*-palm; 8 willow trees; 10 tamarisk trees; 5 *twn*-trees (a kind of acacia?); 2 myrtle(?) (*ḫt-ds*); and 5 unidentified kinds of tree.

The main task of a gardener would have been to keep the plants and trees well watered. To this end he made use of a *shadûf*, a contraption still used in the Egyptian countryside, consisting of a long pole balanced over a stand. To one end is fixed a bucket or jar, to the other a counterpoise of mud. With this implement the field labourer or gardener can scoop up water from the river or canal to the field above without having to lift the heavy pot. In ancient times the beds for utility plants and flowers were divided into squares by grooves so that the water could be poured in at one end and run freely to the far end of the flower

The house and garden of the builder Ineni. Wall-painting in his tomb at Thebes (no. 81); 18th Dynasty. After a drawing by H. Boussac who omitted the fruits of the trees.

Gardeners among persea, sycamore fig, cornflowers, mandrake and poppies. In the pond are blue and white lotus flowers. Wall-painting in a Theban Tomb no. 217; Ramesside.

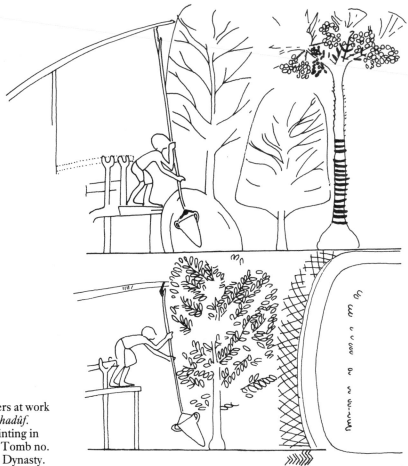

Gardeners at work using a *shadûf*. Wall-painting in Theban Tomb no. 49; 18th Dynasty.

bed. The gardeners carried water in jars on a yoke from the main water supply to the flower beds further afield. Thanks to these continuous efforts the Egyptian official would enjoy a colourful spectacle of flowers at different seasons.

It is interesting to observe the choice of flowers in the garden, insofar as these can be identified. It is hardly surprising to find the beautiful scented lotus floating in the ponds. But the herbaceous border was composed chiefly of flowers which we would expect to find growing in the field: the poppy and the cornflower. A third conventional plant, of similar outline and proportion, is the mandrake, which must have appealed to artist and gardener alike for its decorative yellow fruits which contrast so well with the red and blue of the poppy and cornflower. All three were used together, with lotus and papyrus, in formal bouquets. The Egyptians knew of several other plants which could have been chosen for their ornamental qualities, such as iris, lily, chrysanthemum, and delphinium, but these flowers, so essential to a well-stocked English garden, do not feature in the garden scenes as depicted by the artists.

Exotic plants and trees were much appreciated by the Egyptians, and some imported species did well on Egyptian soil. The pomegranate is a good example of an ornamental garden tree, whose fruits were also put to good use. The olive may have taken longer to become established. An ancient love poem speaks of a fig-tree having been brought from the land of Kharu (Syria) as a trophy of love to be planted in an Egyptian garden. Queen Hatshepsut attempted to transplant incense trees from Punt to the garden of her temple at Deir el-Bahari, but it is doubtful whether the experiment was successful. Tuthmosis III, her successor, showed similar horticultural interests during his exploits into Asia Minor. In order to leave a more permanent record than the plants themselves, which may not even have survived the journey home, he commissioned his artists to draw them and had the pictures carved in relief on the walls of a small room in the temple of Amun at Karnak, now known as 'the Botanical Garden'. This is probably the oldest herbal in the world, but regrettably without an explanatory text to accompany the illustrations.

We are left to speculate about the gardens of the royal palaces, for they were not depicted in the tombs of members of the royal family. But we do have two

Cornflower, poppy and mandrake – a popular trio in Egyptian gardens. Wall-painting in Theban Tomb no. 1; 19th Dynasty.

pictures showing Tutankhamun and his wife in a garden setting. The scenes were carved on the ivory panels of a casket found in the king's tomb. The lid shows the royal couple standing in front of a shelter provided with large cushions and decorated with flowers. The queen hands the king two splendid bouquets, made up of papyrus, lotus and poppy. The scene is framed by a border of poppy, cornflower and mandrake; another scene below shows two more members of the family picking poppy and mandrake. On the front of the casket the king is seated next to the fishpond, aiming at either the fishes or the birds with his bow and arrow. The queen is at his feet, and the scene is idyllic, the garden being densely planted with the by now familiar species.

The oldest temple garden of which we have exact information is one planted in the reign of Mentuhotpe I at his mortuary temple beneath the cliffs at Deir el-Bahari (c. 1975 BC). We are in the unique position of having not only the remains of the tree pits themselves, but also part of the plan drawn up by the landscape architect in charge, sketched on one of the floor slabs of the temple. Three rows of seven sycamore and tamarisk trees were planted on either side of the entrance ramp leading to the temple. Under each tree was positioned a statue of the king. Remains of the trees, including large cuttings of sycamore, were found in the pits, which, when the light is favourable, can easily be distinguished as depressions in the sand.

There is evidence of trees having been planted in pits near other royal funerary monuments, such as for example at the pyramid of Sesostris II at Illahûn. But it is not until we come to the New Kingdom that we get a more accurate picture of temple gardens. Sennufer, the mayor of Thebes in the reign of Amenophis II (c. 1425 BC) had a picture painted in his tomb chapel showing the garden of the temple at Amun as it looked in his day. The garden was conveniently laid out next to the river or a canal. A neat plan shows the walled

Plants from the 'Botanical Garden' in the temple of Amun at Karnak; 18th Dynasty.

Tutankhamun and his queen. Carved ivory panel on a casket from the king's tomb; 18th Dynasty. Egyptian Museum, Cairo.

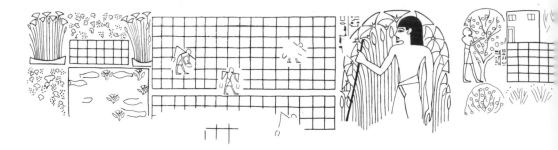

(*Above*) The nursery garden of Amun. Wall-painting in tomb of Nakht at Thebes (no. 161), after a drawing by Hay; 18th Dynasty. British Library (Hay MSS 29822, 96).

garden with its four ponds, with the trees, plants and buildings drawn in elevation, following the Egyptian convention. To the right is the main gate, erected by Amenophis II and inscribed with his names. To the left there is a chapel with three juxtaposed shrines, represented one above the other. Next to two of the ponds a pavilion is depicted. The garden itself is divided into sections by walls and gates, so that the general effect would have been one of intimacy rather than of splendour. The central part is taken up by the god's vineyard, with the vines trained on railings and supports. The garden contained date-palms and *dôm*-palms, and the clumps of papyrus are easy to make out. Among the remaining trees are figs and sycamore. A closer examination of the tomb wall itself might provide more clues to the identity of the other trees, but the tomb is not easily accessible, and the painting itself has deteriorated and is difficult to photograph. The scene was copied in colour by early travellers to Egypt in the second and third decades of the last century.

Among the gods of the Egyptian pantheon none was in a better position to enjoy the efforts of the temple gardeners than Aten, the sun disk who cast his rays over all gardens. In the city built by Akhenaten and Nefertiti on virgin soil at el-Amarna (*c.*1367–1350 BC) a garden was an integral part of the temple complex. The Amarna artists were unusually clever at depicting architecture and surroundings, the otherwise weak point of Egyptian draughtsmanship. A large representation on the wall of the tomb of Meryre, high priest of the Aten, demonstrates in excellent fashion the lay-out of the garden of the sun-god. Inside the large enclosure wall and adjacent to the main temple were a number of buildings interspersed with trees in tubs. The largest of the buildings consisted of numerous storerooms built on either side of a rectangular court with trees. Each half was divided into two by another courtyard onto which the storerooms opened. Their doors were sheltered by a portico with papyrus-shaped columns, and in front of each was a tree. The remaining buildings had similar arrangements of rooms, courts and trees in tubs, but trees were also

16

planted among the houses. Two small and one large pond provided water and variety. Among the trees can be seen flowering pomegranates, dates, *dôm*-palms and vines. It was at the time that this garden was planted that almonds and olives first appeared in Egypt, but not necessarily in the form of actual trees.

Gardens such as these were created to delight the god, and were undoubtedly enjoyed by the staff of the temple as well. The vast quantity of herbs and flowers used for a variety of purposes in the daily cult would probably have been collected from adjacent fields. An enormous number of bouquets were required for the offering tables and a well-organised industry was essential to supply them. One of the men in charge during the reign of Amenophis III (*c.*1375 BC) was Nakht, 'gardener of the divine offerings of Amun', that is to say chief florist of the temple. His tomb in the Theban necropolis appropriately depicts the most splendid bouquets made in Egypt. But like many officials Nakht desired to be depicted 'in office', and he is shown strolling in the nurseries of the god, inspecting the flower beds and watching the gardeners struggling with their yokes and heavy water pots. Although utility gardens had been depicted in tombs since the Old Kingdom, this temple nursery scene is unique. Like the painting of the temple garden of Amenophis II, this one was copied by an early traveller in the 1820s. The scene belongs on the lower part of a wall, and the fragile layer of painted plaster has been rubbed off by visitors over the past 160 years so that little now remains.

Information about a herb garden of a slightly later date comes from a totally different yet equally fragile source. The evidence is contained in three samples of 1cc each of tissue taken from the mummy of King Ramesses II (died 1224 BC). It would seem that during the course of the process of mummification the embalmers of the king used a certain plant of the genus *Compositae*. The plant may have been employed to scent the oil used for anointing the corpse rather than having been applied in its natural state, in which case recognisable fragments would have survived. While the plant was still growing it had attracted samples of pollen from other plants brought either by the wind or by insects. By analysing the samples the pollen could be identified, thus providing clues about the habitat of the plant and the kind of herbs which grew in its vicinity.

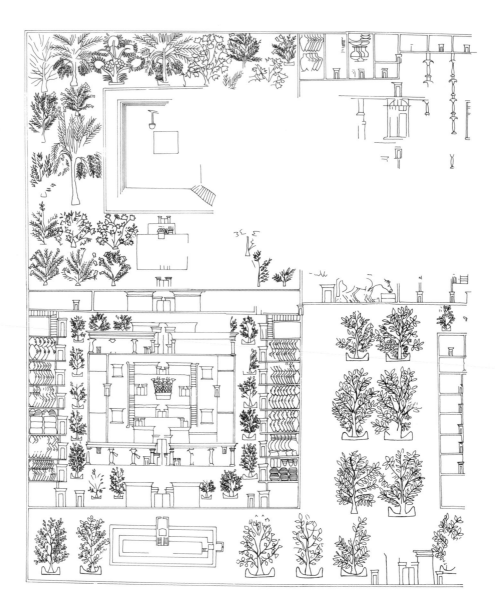

It has been suggested that the plant in question could be a camomile, and that the body of Ramesses II had been anointed with 'camomile oil' (this was a commodity used more than a thousand years later by the Copts). Its identity may not have been established beyond question, but there is less doubt about the origin of the pollen it attracted. The plant grew near a field of emmer or wheat, but at some distance from the river or a canal, for no pollen of plants growing in water was found. Nor was there a palm tree in the neighbourhood. Shade in the area was provided by lime (*Tilia tormentosa*), plane (*Platanus orientalis*), Christ thorn and a fair number of *Phillyrea* bushes. Surprisingly, the garden contained a

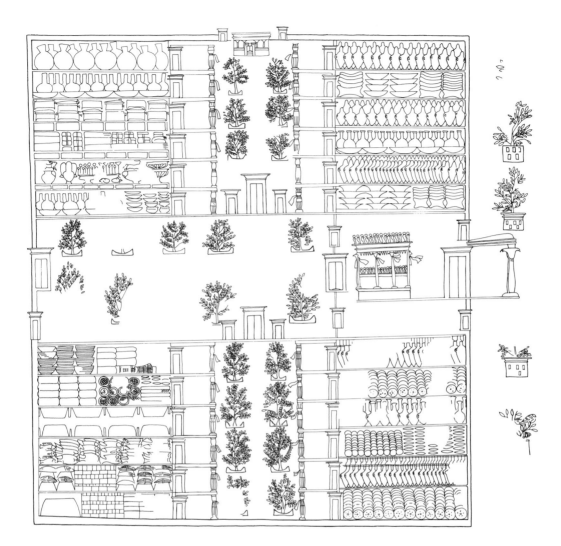

Reliefs from the tomb of Meryre at el-Amarna, showing the gardens of the temple of the Aten; 18th Dynasty.

(*Above*) The storerooms, with trees planted in tubs and pockets of soil. The tree in the top right-hand corner is probably an olive.

(*Opposite page*) The ponds and a small shrine surrounded by storerooms.

cotton plant (*Gossypium*), otherwise only known much later in Egypt. Among the plants known from other gardens (cf. the herbal section below) was hemp, cornflower, wormwood, chicory, convolvulus, nettles and umbelliferous plants. Plantain and sage, not known from other pharaonic sources, were also present. The evidence seems to point to either a garden planted with medicinal herbs, or, alternatively, a 'camomile' field full of weeds! Considering the Egyptians' highly developed pharmacopoiea they must have had 'physics gardens', most likely in connection with a temple, for it was among the priests that knowledge of the medicinal properties of plants was concentrated. During recent excavations in the sacred animal necropolis at Saqqâra an ancient rubbish dump revealed the presence of a variety of medicinal herbs, among others basil, myrtle, henbane, chrysanthemum, acacia, Egyptian plum, pomegranate, apricot, olive, flax and *Withania somnifera*. It would seem that at some stage these herbs had simply been dumped, perhaps to be replaced by fresh supplies. The remains of this interesting discovery are now in the museum at Kew Gardens.

The man in charge of the medicinal plants used by the embalmers of Ramesses II may just possibly be known to us, although strictly speaking the oil could have come from any location in Egypt. The Delta was rich in gardens, but the pollen told us that the 'camomile' grew at some distance from the water. The mortuary temple of Ramesses II is some three kilometres from the river at Thebes, although there were a number of canals in antiquity as now to conduct the water inland. The inspector of gardens of this particular temple was a certain Nezemger, who had his tomb cut and decorated in the plain near by. The paintings have not survived well, but on one wall we can make out Nezemger standing in his office in the garden. The entrance pylon to the temple was shown to the far left. To the rear (right) in the garden was a duckpond, *shadûf*, palms and other trees. Each would have been planted in a pocket of soil, since we are at the edge of the desert.

The garden of the Ramesseum, the mortuary temple of Ramesses II. Wall-painting in the tomb of Nezemger at Thebes (no. 138), after a drawing by M. Baud.

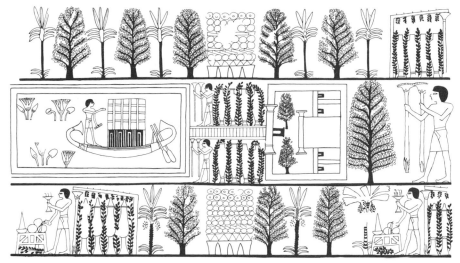

The garden for the funerary ceremonies of Minnakht. Wall-painting in his tomb at Thebes (no. 87); 18th Dynasty.

The funerary ceremonies of private individuals included episodes set in a garden – at least this was the ideal situation as represented on the tomb walls. In his tomb at Thebes a granary official, Minnakht (*c.* 1450 BC), shows his coffin being placed on a boat and sailing across a pond to a garden chapel where it is met by men carrying papyrus stems. Booths placed among the trees contain jars of provisions, while loaves are stacked up in the open, waiting for the priests to consecrate them.

The Egyptians were able to create gardens in the most unlikely places. All they needed was to be able to bring the life-giving Nile water to the chosen location. Irrigation of the desert being undertaken today demonstrates how successful the results can be. The garden of Akhenaten and Nefertiti has now merged with the surrounding desert, but only through lack of water and attention. Even in the remote southern part of the Egyptian empire the temples did not lack gardens. A location called Kawa, near modern Dongola, once boasted the best vineyard in Egypt: its wine was even better than that from the Oasis of Bahriya which was otherwise known to produce wine of quality. The walled garden was planted by Taharqa, a Nubian king of Egypt in the eighth century BC. The famous vines were tended by gardeners from the tribe of the Mentiu in Asia. So we should imagine the length of Egypt planted with beautiful gardens, parks and vineyards. But like the modern Egyptians the ancient inhabitants of the Nile Valley kept their gardens hidden and secluded behind high brick walls.

Bouquets, garlands and collars

The Egyptians were inordinately fond of flowers, which they valued not only for their beauty, but also for sacred and symbolic qualities which they were felt to possess. Single branches might be waved as a sign of high spirits; a scene from a Theban tomb, for example, shows rejoicing women going through the streets with their tambourines and waving acacia branches to greet their master. Even today Egyptians celebrate festivals, such as the Sham el-Nessim spring feast, with drums and palm branches. Bouquets, garlands and collars of fresh flowers were made for use on religious and festive occasions. The papyrus and the lotus were the most popular flowers for use in bouquets. The blue and white lotus might be used alone in bunches of three or more, or as a single flower, or it might be combined with other flowers in a formal bouquet.

Nakht, the florist, with his finest bouquet. Wall-painting in his tomb at Thebes (no. 161), after a drawing by Hay; 18th Dynasty. British Library (Hay MSS 29851, 12–15).

Rejoicing ladies playing tambourines and waving acacia(?) branches. Wall-painting in Theban Tomb no. 49; 18th Dynasty.

Carrying papyrus stems and fruit to the tomb. Wall-painting in Theban Tomb no. 55; 18th Dynasty.

The following method reconstructs an Egyptian formal bouquet:

1. Take a bundle of rushes, palm branches or three papyrus plants cut off at the base to keep the stems as long as possible. Tie them together to form a firm core for the bouquet.

2. Have ready a selection of additional plants, for example lotus, poppy and cornflowers, with their stalks, and mandrake fruits, keeping as much stalk as possible. Tie these to the core in tiers, the smaller items filling the space between the larger ones, giving a compact effect.

3. Make collars of papyrus 'paper' painted red and fasten these to conceal the bindings. For a special effect a pattern of white lotus petals may be painted on the collars. Alternatively real floral garlands can be tied around the core.

A bouquet in the shape of an *ankh*, the sign of life, can be fashioned by first shaping the core from a bundle of rush or straw, then inserting the flowers and concealing the bindings with collars of papyrus.

Floral bouquets played a major part in the cult of the gods. The king would institute offerings to ensure a regular presentation. A list of the contributions of Ramesses III to three of the most important temples is impressive:

Item	Temple of Amun total 1057 days (just under 3 years)	Temple of Re total 23 years	Temple of Re total 31 years	Temple of Ptah total 3 years
Fan bouquets	124			
Tall bouquets	3,100			
Scented bouquets	15,500			
Bouquets	1,975,800	1,150,000	114,804	21,000
Flower bundles	1,975,800	1,150,000	114,805	2,100
Wreaths	60,450	46,000	43,640	2,970
Flowers	620			
Blue flowers on strings	12,400			
Flowers ('hands')	465,000			
Flowers ('heaps')	110			
Lotus ('hands')	144,720	46,000		
Lotus bouquets	3,410			
Small lotus flowers ('hands')	110,000			
Large lettuce and flower bouquets	19,150			

Man presenting a large composite
bouquet. Wall-painting in Theban
Tomb A16 (now lost), after a drawing
by Hay; Ramesside. British Library
(Hay MSS 29851, 138–9).

In return for all these splendid flower arrangements the king expected the gods to grant protection and a long reign.

Bouquets were presented to deceased relatives both on the day of the burial and on any festive occasions celebrated in the necropolis. At Thebes during the Feast of the Valley the statue of the god Amun was carried in procession from his temple at Karnak on the east bank of the river to the tombs on the west bank. The priests carried the divine image up and down the paths among the tombs before arriving at the beautiful temple built by Queen Hatshepsut below the steep cliffs at Deir el-Bahari. The inhabitants of Thebes followed the procession and took the opportunity of gathering at the tombs and presenting the 'bouquet of Amun' to their ancestors. The occasion is often referred to in the tombs of the 18th Dynasty.

Bouquets were among the funerary equipment brought to the tomb on the day of the burial. Stems of papyrus were an essential component for they symbolised the resurrection of the deceased. When the mummy was set upright before the entrance to the tomb for the final rites, a composite bouquet was placed beside it, and was probably buried with the coffin: in the tomb of Tutankhamun were several bouquets, mainly made up of persea branches.

Garlands and collars were also used in the funeral ceremonies. As real flowers would have stayed fresh for a limited time, for funerary use some Egyptians preferred collars with floral motifs made of faience beads shaped like fruits, leaves, petals and pods. Ancient collars of fresh flowers have been found on

(*Above left*) A composite flower arrangement decorating a papyrus column from the *Book of the Dead* of Kha; 18th Dynasty. Museo Egizio, Turin.

(*Above right*) A bouquet replacing the tomb-owner in the offering ritual. Relief in Theban Tomb no. 57; 18th Dynasty.

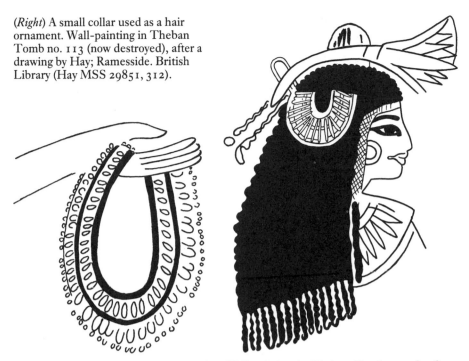

(*Right*) A small collar used as a hair ornament. Wall-painting in Theban Tomb no. 113 (now destroyed), after a drawing by Hay; Ramesside. British Library (Hay MSS 29851, 312).

(*Above*) A servant holding a floral collar. Wall-painting in Theban Tomb no. 38, after a drawing by Hay; 18th Dynasty. British Library (Hay MSS 29853, 180).

mummies and draped around statuettes in the tombs. With care and patience such desiccated flowers can be moistened and pressed and restored to give a good impression of their original appearance.

The coffins of Tutankhamun were bedecked with a number of floral ornaments at his burial in 1339 BC. It is interesting to note that, judging by the choice of flowers, the ceremony must have taken place between mid-March and the end of April. A small wreath was placed around the vulture and serpent decorating the king's brow on the second golden coffin. It consisted of olive leaves, petals of blue lotus and heads of cornflower bound together over a strip of papyrus and held in place by two thin strands of papyrus passing over and under the leaves. The olive leaves were arranged with every alternate leaf upside down, so that the silvery upper surfaces contrasted with the dark green lower ones. This simple ornament of blue and green must have been very effective against the golden coffin with its blue inlaid eyes and eyebrows.

The innermost coffin was covered with a linen shroud which was adorned with garlands in four rows. The first two were made up of olive leaves and cornflower; the third of willow leaves, cornflower heads and blue lotus petals; and the fourth of olive leaves, cornflower heads and celery leaves on a base of papyrus.

A splendid broad collar was found below the linen shroud, resting on the third

27

(*Left*) The small collar on Tutankhamun's brow. Egyptian Museum, Cairo.

(*Below*) The shroud and garlands over Tutankhamun's innermost golden coffin. Egyptian Museum, Cairo.

(*Right*) The mummy garlands of Ramesses II as drawn by Schweinfurth.

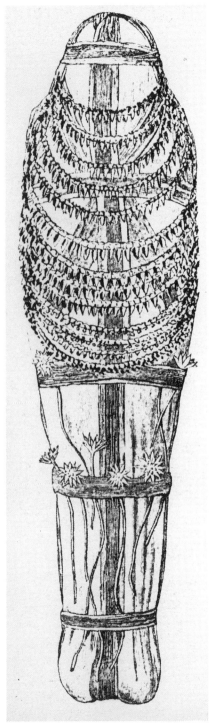

and innermost golden coffin. It was an elaborate composition of blue glass beads and fresh flowers, arranged in nine rows on a semi-circular base of papyrus:

1. Groups of 20–22 glass beads + 4 berries of woody nightshade, fastened to strips of date leaf.

2. As 1.

3. As 1.

4. Willow leaves + an unidentified plant, forming clasps for petals of blue lotus.

5. Berries of woody nightshade on strips of date leaf.

6. Cornflower heads + heads of *Picris coronopifolia* Asch. + the same unidentified plant as in row 4 + 11 halved mandrake fruits spaced out on the string and sewn onto the papyrus base.

7. As 1.

8. Alternating leaves of olive and the unidentified plant.

9. Cornflower heads + the unidentified plant.

Contrasting with the previous garlands, this collar would have been a colourful spectacle of blue beads, lotus and cornflower, scarlet berries of nightshade, and the yellow of *Picris* and mandrake. The plants must have been chosen mainly for their decorative qualities, as it is difficult to find any other common denominator.

Other collars connected with Tutankhamun had actually been found in the Valley of the Kings some fifteen years before the tomb itself was discovered. It seems that a funerary banquet took place at the burial, and some of the participants, who had dined on beef, goose and duck, wore floral collars. Along with materials used in the embalming of the king, these remains were buried in the desert. The collars were not unlike the one described above, but less complex, consisting of olive leaves, cornflowers and woody nightshade on a base of papyrus. They are now in the Metropolitan Museum in New York.

The mummy of Ramesses II (1290–1224 BC) yielded thirteen rows of floral garlands and a number of single blue lotus flowers stuck under the bands sealing the mummy wrappings. The king's coffin was removed from its tomb in the Valley of the Kings along with several other royal mummies around 1087 BC and reburied in another tomb. This second mass burial remained undisturbed until the end of the nineteenth century, and the floral decorations of the mummies presumably date from the time of the reburial.

The garlands of Ramesses II appear to be more or less identical, consisting of persea leaves and petals of blue and white lotus. G. Schweinfurth (1836–1925), the botanist who pioneered research into ancient Egyptian plant material, left a drawing of the garlands which is so accurate that we can give step-by-step instructions as to how to make such a garland. The physical remains of the ornaments are now in the Agricultural Museum in Cairo and the Herbier du Museé de Paris.

The broad collar on Tutankhamun's innermost coffin. Egyptian Museum, Cairo.

To make a floral garland:

1. Make a string by twisting together fibres of palm leaves.

2. Take a quantity of lotus petals and persea leaves. Leave some 20 inches of the string free at either end to use for tying the collar.

3. Fold a persea leaf one third of the distance from the top. Fold once more one third further down and fasten the leaf over the string. Fold the remaining third of the leaf to make a neat edge. This will be the front of the collar.

4. Insert a lotus petal in the persea leaf so that about half the petal is visible.

5. Stitch with date-palm fibre.

6. Take the next persea leaf and arrange as the first, but overlapping slightly. Insert another lotus petal, and continue until the required length of garland has been achieved.

7. For a broad collar prepare another garland of lotus and persea and fasten to the first so that the upper row overlaps slightly.

The garland chosen for the mummy of Ahmosi (1575–1550 BC), reburied with the other royal mummies, shows a novel combination of willow leaves, blue lotus and flowers of larkspur (*Delphinium orientale*), a plant known from other sources in Egypt, though little has been recorded of its use other than as an ornament. Red poppies were included in some mummy garlands belonging to a princess Nesikhonsu, whereas others were made of willow leaves and the unpretentious *Picris* which we saw in the garlands of Tutankhamun.

Garlands decorating an offering table. Wall-painting in Theban Tomb no. 113 (now destroyed), after a drawing by Hay; Ramesside. British Library (Hay MSS 29822, 121).

About the home

Apart from their purely decorative qualities, plants and flowers had many uses about the home. They could, for example, help to ward off infestation by vermin. Insects and rodents were all too frequent visitors to the house: at Illahûn in Middle Egypt, one of the few town sites to have survived at all, the houses were found to have been tunnelled in every corner by rodents. The holes they had made had been blocked with stones and rubbish in an attempt to keep the intruders out. Mice were a particular problem, which is one reason why Egyptians kept cats and why, in representations, these animals always look well fed. Failing a cat, 'cat's grease' was placed on all things which were likely to attract rodents.

Dangerous snakes would find their way into houses in the country. If a snake's nest was discovered, the reptile was prevented from leaving it by a dried fish or some lumps of natron placed at the hole; an onion might serve the same purpose.

Fleas were a constant nuisance, and the housewife tried to keep them at bay by sprinkling the house with natron water. Another efficient remedy was to grind fleabane (*Inula* spp.) with charcoal, and to dust the house thoroughly with it. If the use of these ancient disinfectants gave the house an unpleasant smell, a number of ingredients, including frankincense, myrrh, cinnamon bark and several unidentified plants, might be mixed with honey, boiled and shaped into pellets. These were used to fumigate the house, but in addition left a pleasant smell in the clothes, and could also be used as a masticatory to sweeten the breath.

Some remedies were felt to require the benefit of magic to make them effective:

To prevent the kite from robbing: a branch of acacia. Let it stand up. You shall say: 'Oh Horus, he has stolen in the town and in the field, his thirst is for the birds' field; he shall be cooked and eaten. It is recited over a branch of acacia, and the cakes are applied to it. This is the way to prevent the kite from robbing. (E 848)

A man with pellets of incense. Relief in a tomb at Memphis, after a drawing by G. T. Martin; 19th Dynasty. Römer-Pelizäus Museum, Hildesheim (1873).

33

Plants supplied the raw materials for many everyday objects used about the home. Various utensils in the kitchen, such as baskets and sieves, would be made from plant fibres. Jars for provisions had saucer-like lids or stoppers made either of barley chaff glued together or a parcel of young sycamore leaves. On festive occasions wine jars were provided with herbal stoppers and draped with garlands of vine leaves and other plants. Sprigs of herbs were used to pack fragile eggs or decorate cone-shaped sweetmeats, and loaves have been found packed with sycamore leaves or wrapped in bands of papyrus.

Vegetable materials were also used in lighting. In ordinary homes lamps consisted of a simple pottery bowl with a wick floating in oil; in royal palaces and

A boat in a funeral cortege, loaded with provisions protected by herbs. Wall-painting in Theban Tomb no. 49; 18th Dynasty.

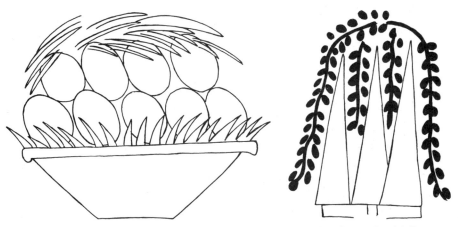

(*Above left*) Pelicans' eggs(?) and herbs. Wall-painting in Theban Tomb no. 78; 18th Dynasty. (*Above right*) Conical loaves and herbs. Wall-painting in Theban Tomb no. 38, after a drawing by Hay; 18th Dynasty. British Library (Hay MSS 29851, 275).

34

The double calcite lamp from the tomb of Tutankhamun at Thebes. Egyptian Museum, Cairo.

wealthier homes lamps would be more elaborate, perhaps made from semi-translucent calcite. Candles were also used in the home and by sculptors and painters at work in the temples and tombs. Candlewicks were made of fibre steeped in vegetable oil or animal fat, and would have burnt like torches. Sesame oil is frequently recorded as having been used for candles. The use of animal fat, such as ox tallow, allowed candles to be moulded into shapes. Some of those used to light the tombs during the funerary ceremonies were large cones fixed to a stick, and were often dyed and decorated with garlands; the final impression was not unlike that of a modern Christmas decoration.

Candles were used by the workmen from Deir el-Medîna, who built the royal tombs of Thebes. Raw materials were supplied for them to make their candles at home, with the help of their relatives. Accurate records were kept of how much material was issued and how many candles were burnt each day to provide light for the work in the tomb. On one specific day, for example, the 16th day of the 4th month of the inundation season, a total of 58 candles had been burnt.

These candles might have been expected to have given off a substantial amount of smoke, but no traces of it survive on the painted walls of the tombs. Herodotus records that the Egyptians of his time, the fifth century BC, added salt to their lamp oil. Salt would absorb any trace of water which might have caused the candle to smoke, and, indeed, salt was used for this very purpose as late as the nineteenth century in Egypt. It is also possible that the Egyptians used to burn scented oils. A lamp found in the tomb of Kha at Deir el-Medîna still contained the remains of fat along with a lump of a substance as yet unidentified, which may be some odiferous material.

Dyeing cloth and matting was a skill developed by the Egyptians more than

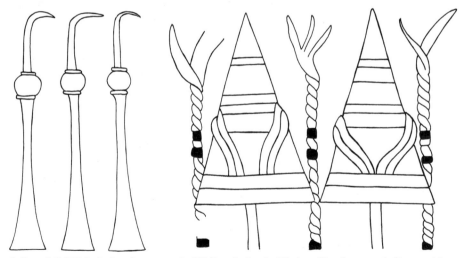

(*Above left*) Wicks in bowls on stands. Wall-painting in Theban Tomb no. 276; Ramesside.
(*Above right*) Torches and candles. Wall-painting in Theban Tomb no. 51; Ramesside.

Dyeing cloth in a vat. Wall-painting from a Theban tomb; 18th Dynasty. Museo Egizio, Turin.

five thousand years ago. The dyes used were obtained from local, natural sources. Red dye was extracted from the roots of *Alkanna tinctoria*, *Rubia tinctorum* (madder) and the flowers of *Carthamus tinctorius*. It is possible that henna was used as well. *Carthamus tinctorius* was also the source of a yellow dye, whereas blue was obtained by fermentation of the leaves of *Indigofera* (woad). Brown and purple were made by imposing madder on woad, or by mixing the threads in weaving. Dyed threads found use in royal garments, such as tunics and gloves, which were woven in beautiful patterns. However, ordinary Egyptians seem to have preferred to keep their linen plain white, at least for clothing. The reason for this may be purely practical in that linen, the most widely used fabric, does not accept dye easily.

The mordant used for fixing the dye was most probably alum, which occurs locally. Pliny describes the Egyptian method of dyeing: 'They employ a very remarkable process for the colouring of tissues. After pressing the material, which is white at first, they saturate it not with colours, but with mordants that are calculated to absorb the colour. This done, the tissues, still unchanged in appearance, are plunged into a cauldron of boiling dye, and are removed the next moment fully coloured. It is a singular fact, too, that although the dye in the pan is of one uniform colour, the material when taken out is of various colours, according to the nature of the mordants that have been respectively added to it: these colours, too, will never wash out' (*NH.* xxxv.xiii).

Apart from dyeing cloth, the Egyptians used to dye leather red, yellow or green. The red colour used appears to have been madder and the yellow pomegranate rind. The nature of green leather dye is not apparent.

In the kitchen

The garden and fields yielded a wide selection of items for the table. Bread, onions and beer formed the staple diet; honey, dates and raisins were used as sweetening agents, and milk, fruit and vegetables provided some proteins and vitamins. The river supplied fish, whereas meat appears to have been a less frequent treat for most people. It was a wholesome diet, which would have helped to ensure good health for anyone with a sufficient and regular supply. There were, however, many health hazards in ancient Egypt, which not even a healthy diet could ward off: pollution caused by man himself, cramped living quarters, multiple use of water in canals and pools, and ignorance of the causes of contamination.

Clues about diet can be gained by examining the contents of the stomachs of well-preserved bodies. However, although Egyptian mummies are admirably preserved, the process of embalming involved the removal of the stomach, along with the other organs in the abdomen. Before the days of artificial mummifi-

The gift of the tree goddess: loaves, figs, a pomegranate, a cucumber(?), grapes and a honeycomb. Wall-painting in Theban Tomb no. 51; Ramesside.

A table of offerings including: meat, fowl, loaves, cucumbers(?), fruit, honeycombs, lotus flowers; below are wine jars and above unguents. Wall-painting from the Theban tomb of Nebamun; 18th Dynasty. British Museum (37985).

Selling herbs in the market. Wall-painting in Theban Tomb no. 54; Ramesside.

cation, bodies were left to dry in the sand with the organs intact, and some of these early Egyptians were found to have eaten a meal of barley, presumably in the form of bread, shortly before they died.

The tombs themselves can sometimes supply fascinating information. The tomb of Kha at Deir el-Medîna is one of the few to have survived intact until modern times. Like most of the inhabitants of Deir el-Medîna, Kha was involved in cutting and decorating the royal Theban tombs around 1400 BC. Among the many interesting finds in his tomb was a rich supply of provisions from which may be learnt something of the regular requirements of an Egyptian official of rank. Kha and his wife were given a large selection of loaves of bread, jars of wine, vessels containing flour, fat and milk, plucked and salted fowl, salted chunks of meat, dried fish, a bowl of shredded vegetables with gravy or dressing, a wooden jug of kitchen salt, bunches of garlic and onion, bowls of dates, raisins and persea fruits, and a selection of spices, such as juniper berries and cumin seeds. They would have been able to enjoy many a good meal in the Hereafter using these ingredients.

As no ancient Egyptian cookery books have survived, our notions of how the

A basket of fruits: melons(?), figs and dates. Relief from a tomb at Memphis, after a drawing by G. T. Martin; 19th Dynasty. Pittsburgh (72. 18. 1).

Egyptians prepared their food are mostly conjectural. The medical prescriptions read almost like present-day cookery recipes, and it may just be a matter of time until a fragment of a pharaonic cookery book is discovered. The closest we can get is the classical 'Apicius', a collection of recipes put together in Rome in the first century AD. Other classical authors contribute with scattered references to Egyptian eating habits. The Apicius cookery book quotes some Alexandrian recipes, and although these are probably very different from those of pharaonic times, they are the only precise indications of food preparation in Egypt in ancient times.

Alexandrian marrows

[First prepare the sauce:] Pound pepper, cumin, coriander seed, fresh mint, asafoetida root. Moisten with *liquamen**. Add Jericho dates, pine kernels and mash well. Blend with honey, vinegar, [more] *liquamen*, *defrutum** and oil. Boil the marrows, sprinkle with salt and arrange in a shallow pan. Pour the sauce over the marrows. Bring them to the boil, sprinkle with pepper and serve. (Apicius III.iv.3)

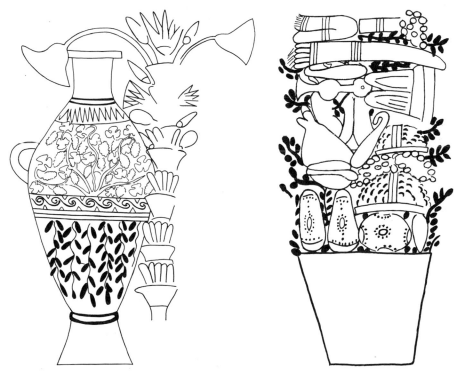

(*Above left*) Decorated wine jar. Wall-painting in a Theban Tomb, after a drawing by Hay; 18th Dynasty. British Library (Hay MSS 29853, 166–7).

(*Above right*) A basket of bread, meat, fruit, vegetables and herbs. Wall-painting from a Theban Tomb; 18th Dynasty. Ägyptisches Museum, East Berlin (18528).

Alexandrian sauce for grilled fish I

[Blend] lovage, cumin, oregano, celery seed, stoned damsons, *mulsum*,* vinegar, *liquamen*, *defrutum* and oil. Boil gently.

Alexandrian sauce for grilled fish II

[Blend] pepper, lovage, fresh coriander, stoned raisins, wine, *passum*,* *liquamen* and oil. Boil gently.

Alexandrian sauce for grilled fish III

[Blend] pepper, lovage, fresh coriander, onion, stoned damsons, *passum*, *liquamen*, vinegar and oil. Boil gently. (Apicius x.i.6–8)

Stuffed Alexandrian loaf

Hollow out an Alexandrian loaf and sprinkle with water mixed with vinegar. Grind in a mortar pepper, honey, mint, garlic, fresh coriander, salted cow's milk cheese, water and oil.
Fill the loaf with [cooked] chicken meat and goat's sweetbreads, hard cheese, pine kernels, diced cucumber and finely chopped dried onion. Pour the dressing over. Cool in the snow and serve.
An alternative filling: cow's milk cheese, diced cucumber, pine kernels, capers, [cooked] chicken liver. (Apicius iv.i.1, 3)

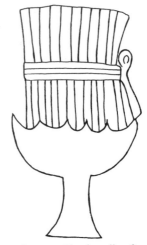

A vase with a bundle of herbs. Wall-painting in Theban Tomb no. 38, after a drawing by Hay; 18th Dynasty. British Library (Hay MSS 29853, 173).

According to Pliny (*NH*.xv.lviii) Alexandrian bread was flavoured with cumin.

* *liquamen:* a common condiment used by the Romans, based on salted fish. Worcester sauce or Shoyu/Tamari may be substituted by modern cooks.
defrutum: must reduced by boiling.
mulsum: wine mixed with honey.
passum: a sweet wine used for cooking.

Although scenes of cooking are not infrequently represented on the walls of tombs of the pharaonic period they rarely depict the preparation of the ingredients included in this book. The tomb of Rekhmire, vizier of King

Preparing tiger nuts. Wall-painting in Theban Tomb no. 100; 18th Dynasty.

Tuthmosis III in the fifteenth century BC, provides the exception. Among Rekhmire's many duties was the supervision of the preparations of certain loaves destined for the offering tables of the gods in the first place, but eventually consumed by the priests or recycled among the population of Thebes. The ingredients are being brought into the treasury under the watchful eye of the vizier, while the texts tell us that the loaves are being made as a special offering instituted by the king for every feast anew. They were prepared from the ground tubers of *Cyperus esculentus* L., commonly know as 'tiger nuts'. The flour was produced on the premises of the treasury, but the remaining preparations were carried out in the 'sweets' room', the patisserie. Perhaps we can attempt to read the recipe from the pictures on the wall:

Tiger nut sweets

1. Grind a quantity of tiger nuts in a mortar.

2. Sift the flour carefully.

3. To the ground tiger nuts add a bowl of honey and mix to a dough.

4. Transfer the dough to a shallow metal(?) vessel. Place on top of the fire and add a little fat. [Boil over a gentle fire until a firm paste is obtained. It must smell toasted, not burnt.]

5. [Cool and] shape into tall conical loaves.

Among the more unusual items which graced the table of the ancient Egyptians was lotus bread. This was observed by Herodotus (II.92) and Theophrastus (IV.8.11), the latter describing how the ripe heads of the white lotus were left to decay. After this they were washed in Nile water; the fruit, which resembled millet, was extracted and left to dry. It was then pounded and the flour made into loaves. Pliny adds that the dough was kneaded with milk and water, and that when hot the loaves were light and easily digestible (*NH*.XXII. xxviii). The root of the plant was also eaten. It was round and about the size of a quince, enclosed in a black 'bark'. The inside was white, but when boiled and roasted it turned the colour of eggyolk, and became sweet. The root could also be eaten raw, but was less palatable. The delicacy was known as *korsion* (Theophrastus IV.8.11).

Pliny also enumerates fifteen other plants eaten by the Egyptians in his *Natural History* (XXI.liv) but these have not been identified.

Cosmetics

Cleanliness and personal appearance were highly regarded by the ancient Egyptians. For the priests in the service of the gods cleanliness was strictly prescribed. Not only did they have to wash several times a day, but they also had to be clean shaven all over, to keep at bay parasites, such as lice, eggs of which have been found in the hair of mummies. Water was plentiful, but there is little evidence that the ancient Egyptians used natural soaps or tooth powder. In a hot climate deodorants were much in demand. To repel body odour men and women alike were advised to rub pellets of ground carob(?) into the skin (E 709), or to place little balls of incense and porridge where limbs met (E 711).

Around 1400 BC three ladies of the court of Tuthmosis III were buried with costly royal funerary equipment, which included cosmetics. Two of the jars contained a cleansing cream made of oil and lime. Some prescriptions for body 'scrub' are given in the medical papyri (for the quantities used in the recipes see p. 63):

Powdered calcite 1; red natron 1; Lower Egyptian salt 1; honey 1; is ground to a paste and rubbed into the body. (H 154 = E 715 = Sm 21,6–8)
Honey 1; red natron 1; Lower Egyptian salt 1; is ground to a paste and rubbed into the body. (H 153 = E 714 = Sm 21,3–6)

The 'red natron' was presumably natron tinted by an iron compound in the earth where the natron was extracted.

An allegedly successful remedy to treat wrinkles consisted of:

gum of frankincense 1; wax 1; fresh moringa oil 1; cyperus grass 1; is ground finely and mixed with fermented plant juice. Apply daily. (E 716)

A lady from the court of Ramesses II, pricking the stem of a plant, presumably to extract its latex. On the basis of its appearance the plant has been identified as hollyhock, but the juice of the stem of this plant is not known to be of cosmetic, medicinal or other use. Painting on a faience tile from the king's residence in the Delta. Egyptian Museum, Cairo (JdE 89483).

A lady wiping her face. Relief of unknown provenance; 11th Dynasty. British Museum (1658).

A simple remedy of gum applied to the face after cleansing had a similar effect (E 717). If the skin was marred by scars caused by burning, a special ointment was used to treat them and make them less obvious, as for example red ochre and *kohl*, ground and mixed with sycamore juice (E 505). An alternative treatment was a bandage of carob(?) and honey (E 506), or an ointment made of frankincense and honey (E 508).

Because of their healthy diet and the lack of sugar the Egyptians did not suffer from tooth decay, but their bread contained particles of sand from the grain and grit from the grinding stone, which caused their teeth to become excessively worn. No evidence has been recovered to suggest that the Egyptians used a toothbrush in the manner of the *miswak*, a natural brush-cum-toothpaste from *Salvadora persica*, a tree native to southern Egypt and the Sudan. The root has been used for dental care by the Muslims since the days of the Prophet. To improve on their breath the Egyptians chewed herbs, or they gargled with milk (E 697). Perhaps they also chewed frankincense like their descendants in the last century.

As in many other civilisations, the appearance of the hair was of paramount importance, not only because of the visual effect, but also because of the erotic symbolism conventionally connected with hair. Men and women alike wore wigs made of human hair on festive occasions, but they also tried to keep their natural hair in good condition. Jars of what could be compared with 'setting lotion' have been found to contain a mixture of beeswax and resin. There were remedies for problems such as baldness and greying hair. To treat the latter, blood of a black ox or calf was boiled in oil to transfer the blackness of the animal to the greying hair, or the black horn of a gazelle was made into an unguent with oil to prevent grey hairs from appearing. These remedies are slightly more agreeable than another consisting of putrid donkey's liver steeped in oil, though they all had the same magic effect. A far more efficient remedy would be an ointment made of juniper berries and two unidentified plants kneaded into a paste with oil and heated (H 147). The natural colouring matter in the plants would rub off on the hair, and the astringent properties of juniper stimulate the scalp. In order to make the hair grow, chopped lettuce was placed on a bald patch, if the baldness occurred after an illness (E 467), or the head was anointed with equal parts of fir oil and another oil or fat (E 473).

The toilet casket of any man or woman would contain a razor for removing body hair, although a number of creams were sometimes used for the purpose. One such consisted of the boiled and crushed bones of a bird, mixed with fly dung, oil, sycamore juice, gum, and cucumber; this mixture would be heated and applied, presumably to be pulled off when cold, with the hair adhering to it (H 155).

The almond shape of the black Egyptian eyes was underlined by the application of black *kohl* or green malachite. Eyepaint was also considered as a treatment to cure or prevent eye diseases. A great number of prescriptions deal with preventing ingrowing eyelashes.

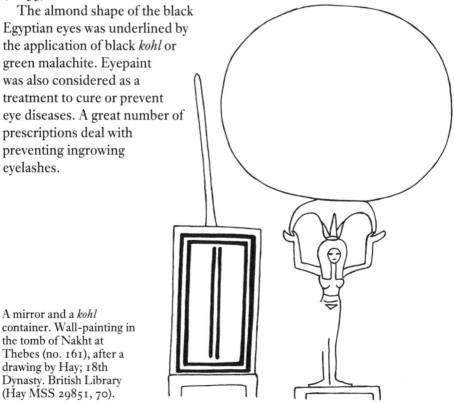

A mirror and a *kohl* container. Wall-painting in the tomb of Nakht at Thebes (no. 161), after a drawing by Hay; 18th Dynasty. British Library (Hay MSS 29851, 70).

To cool the eyes a finely ground green mineral (jasper or serpentine) mixed with water was applied to the lids (Ram III A 24–5). Alternative preparations were ground carob(?) and fermented honey (Ram III A 24–5), or emmer grains steeped in water overnight (Ram III A 25–6). An eye wash was prepared from ground celery and hemp (Ram III A 26).

Eyepaint for an overnight treatment was made of *kohl* and goose fat (E 389), or a paste was mixed from *kohl*, green eyepaint, lapis lazuli, honey and ochre in equal parts, applied to the lids (E 390). The green eyepaint was usually malachite, a green ore of copper; *kohl* was made of galena, a dark grey ore of lead. It was kept in lumps in little bags of linen or leather and was ground on a palette to a fine powder. The powder was poured into vases or tube-shaped containers from which it was extracted with a thin stick. It was applied either with the moistened stick, as is done by Egyptian women today, or, for medicinal purposes as quoted above, mixed with some fatty matter.

Malachite was brought to the Nile Valley from the mountainous regions of Sinai, whereas galena was obtained either near Aswân in Upper Egypt or at the Red Sea coast. But both were also imported as luxury commodities from Asia and Arabia. However, no matter which remedy was employed, the Egyptians knew that nothing made the eyes brighter than falling in love: 'Like eyepaint is my desire. When I see you, it makes my eyes sparkle', says a girl in a love poem.

Some Egyptians appear to have dyed their fingernails, but the nature of the red colour used is unknown. It may have been henna. Red was also required to paint the lips. The lip gloss, possibly made of fat with red ochre or with one of the plants used for dyeing, was applied with a brush or spatula. Red colour was used to give glow to the cheeks. A rouge consisting of red ochre and fat, possibly with a little gum resin, has survived: it was some four thousand years old. Rouge in the form of powder was marketed a few years ago as a product of ancient Egyptian origin. The recipe which inspired the manufacturers was presumably one of those used for the purpose of camouflaging a burn.

A lady applying lip gloss. From a Ramesside papyrus. Museo Egizio, Turin.

47

Perfume

Throughout the ancient world the Egyptians were famous for their scents and perfumes. The country was considered the most suitable for the manufacture of such commodities. As the distillation of alcohol was not known until the fourth century BC the scents were extracted by steeping plants, flowers or splinters of fragrant wood in oil to obtain essential oil, which would then be added to other oils or fat. The materials were placed in a piece of cloth which was wrung until the last drop of fragrance had been retrieved. Alternatively they were boiled with oil and water and the oil skimmed off.

The herbs and spices employed will be discussed below under the individual plants. As for the oils, there was a wide choice, the most commonly used being moringa, balanos, castor oil, linseed, sesame, safflower, and, to some extent, almond and olive. According to Theophrastus, who made a thorough study of fragrant substances in an essay entitled *Concerning Odours*, balanos was the least viscous and by far the most suitable oil, followed by fresh raw olive oil and almond oil.

One of the most famous Egyptian 'perfumes' was made in the city of Mendes in the Delta, whence it was exported to Rome. It consisted of balanos oil, myrrh and resin (Pliny, *NH*.XIII.ii). Dioscorides (1.72) adds cassia. The order in which ingredients were added to the oil was important, as the last one imparted the most pungent scent. Theophrastus mentions as an example that if one pound of myrrh is added to half a pint of oil, and at a later stage one third of an ounce of cinnamon was put in, the cinnamon will dominate. The secret of the Egyptian unguent-makers was obviously to know at which precise moment to add the various ingredients, and at which temperature. The Mendesian 'perfume' was known as 'The Egyptian' par excellence. Unlike many others, it was left its natural colour. It had the added advantage of keeping very well: one perfumer in Greece had had a batch in his shop for eight years, and it was even better than the freshly made 'perfume'. Once applied to the skin it lasted well, too. As

Extracting the essence of lilies. Ptolemaic relief. Museo Egizio, Turin (1673).

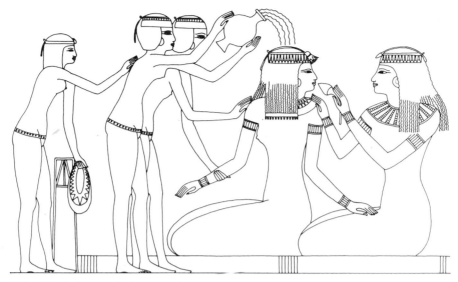

(*Above*) Red ointment being poured over a lady at a banquet. Wall-painting in Theban Tomb no. 77, after a drawing by Prisse d'Avennes; 18th Dynasty.

(*Right*) Carrying unguent jars in the funeral procession. Wall-painting in Theban Tomb no. 55; 18th Dynasty.

Theophrastus said: 'A lasting perfume is what women require'. If 'The Egyptian' was found to be too heavily scented, its strong odour could be lightened by being mixed with sweet wine.

Metopion was the name of another Egyptian ointment, Metopion being, according to Dioscorides, the Egyptian name of the plant from which galbanum was derived. It consisted of oil from bitter almonds and unripe olives scented with cardamom, sweet rush, sweet flag, honey, wine, myrrh, seed of balsamum, galbanum and turpentine resin. The wine apparently entered the preparations either to soak the herbs, or to give a certain 'point' to the ointment. According to Dioscorides the best Metopion was the one that smelt more of cardamom and myrrh than of galbanum. In medicine the ointment was considered generally mollifying, heat- and sweat-producing, and it was used to 'open the vessels', draw and purge ulcers and to treat cut sinews and muscles (Dioscorides I.71; Pliny, *NH*.XIII.ii).

An Egyptian ointment scented with lilies was much esteemed, particularly if the smell of lilies was strong. It was warming and mollifying, and was used to treat 'female' complaints. The preparation was laborious, and large quantities are given:

Bruising herbs(?) for unguents.
Wall-painting in Theban Tomb no. 175.
18th Dynasty.

Oil of Lilies

Mix 9lb 5oz oil, 5lb 3oz sweet flag and 5oz myrrh in scented wine. Boil it together and strain. Bruise and macerate 3lb 6oz cardamom in rain water, and add to the oil. Leave to macerate, then strain. Take one thousand lilies. Strip them of their leaves and place them in a broad and shallow vessel. Pour over 3½lb of the oil. Anoint your hands with honey and use them for stirring the contents of the pot. Leave for 24 hours. Strain, and skim the oil off the water. No water must remain with the oil. Take another vessel and smear the inside with honey. Pour the oil in and sprinkle with a little salt. Remove any impurities as they gather. Set this first batch of oil aside. Take the herbs in the sieve and place them in a vessel. Add another 3½lb of the oil and 1¼oz crushed cardamom, stir with the hands, leave for a while, then strain. [Sprinkle with salt and] remove any dirt and set this second batch aside. Pour the remaining oil over the plants and repeat with cardamom and salt. Set this third batch aside.

Then take again one thousand lilies, strip them of their leaves and pour over the first batch of oil. Repeat with cardamom and salt as before. The more times you repeat with fresh lilies, the stronger the ointment will be. The first batch will be the best.

When the required strength has been obtained take 9oz best myrrh, 1¼oz crocus and 9⅜oz cinnamon (or equal amounts of crocus and cinnamon). Beat and sift it, place it in a vessel with water and pour on it a batch of the lily-scented oil. Leave for a while, [then skim the oil] and store in small pots the inside of which has been coated with gum, or myrrh, and saffron and honey diluted with water. Repeat with the second and third batch. (Dioscorides 1.62)

Gum and resin were added to ointments not only for their own scent, but also to fix the fragrance of other ingredients, just as they are an optional ingredient of potpourri today. Apart from their use in fumigation, frankincense and myrrh were frequently required in medical prescriptions. Frankincense occurs as light yellowish-brown 'tears' on certain trees of the genus *Boswellia* which grow in Southern Arabia and on the Somali coast, or on the *Commiphora pedunculata* in eastern Sudan and Ethiopia. The Egyptians obtained it from the land of Punt, which has not been definitively placed on the map, although it seems most likely to have been in the region of Somalia. Myrrh, consisting of yellowish-red 'tears', is obtained from *Commiphora*. It was also imported from or via Punt. Large quantities of these commodities were needed in Egypt for the daily cult in the temples, in the funerary ritual, and in cosmetics and medicine.

Apart from scented oils and ointments, the Egyptians had thought of another method of perfuming the body. A solid mass of fat, presumably ox tallow, previously perfumed with herbs and spices, was shaped into a cone and fixed to the wig or placed on the crown of the head. During the festivities part of the fat would inevitably soften or even melt and envelop the wig, clothes and body with its grease and scent. This custom may not seem very appetising to modern Western taste, but it nevertheless survived into the present century among certain Beduin tribes who inhabited deserts around Egypt.

Dioscorides gives detailed instructions concerning the manufacture of scented fat:

(*Above left*) Lady with an unguent cone. Wall-painting in Theban Tomb no. 69; 18th Dynasty.

(*Above right*) A young girl with a pot of unguent. Fragment of wall-painting from a tomb at Thebes; 18th Dynasty. Formerly in the de Benzion collection, Cairo.

To make scented ox fat

Remove any blood and skin from the fat. Pour over it some old scented wine. Boil together over a slow fire until the fat has lost its own smell and rather smells of the wine. Remove from the fire and leave to cool. Take out the fat and place in a 17 pint pot. For 2lb fat add 2 pints wine, 4lb Nettle tree seeds [identified as *Celtis australis*, 'the one used for making pipes']. Boil over a slow fire, stirring continuously. When the greasy smell has disappeared, strain and cool.

Take 1lb bruised *aspalathus* [identified as *Cytisus lanigerus*, *Genista acanthoclada*, a shrub used to 'thicken' ointment, or by Theophrastus translators as *Calycotome villosa*] and 4lb *amaracinum* flowers [sweet marjoram?]. Steep them overnight in old wine. Place them in the pot with the fat and 3 pints wine. Boil together. When the fat has absorbed the scent, strain, [cool and skim off the fat] and store. To make the scent even sweeter 1oz of the fattest myrrh, diluted in 'wine of many years' standing', may be added. (Dioscorides II.91)

Straining herbs. Wall-painting in Theban Tomb no. 175; 18th Dynasty.

To make scented goose or pork fat

Place 2 pints clean fat in an earthenware pot. Mix with 1½oz each of *erysisceptrum* [*Cyperus rotondus*], *xylobalsamum* [wood of *Balsamodendron opobalsamum* to 'thicken'], palm shoots, sweet flag, all finely bruised, and 1 cup old wine from Lesbos. Bring to the boil three times, remove and cool for 24 hours. Melt again and sieve through clean linen into a clean pot. When it has set remove it with a spoon to a new pot. Seal and store. This recipe is only successful during the winter, or the mixture will separate. A little wax can be mixed in to counteract this. (Dioscorides II.91)

The Egyptians would probably have used different ingredients from some of those mentioned in these recipes, but the method of preparation must have been very similar.

Dioscorides quotes a recipe for a marjoram unguent called *sampsuchum*. Since he uses the Egyptian plant name it may have been an Egyptian speciality:

Sampsuchum unguent

Take 1lb fat, preferably bull's fat, and 1½lb ripe *sampsuchum* carefully bruised. Mix well and sprinkle with wine. Shape to little cakes. Place in a vessel and leave covered overnight. Next day place the cakes in a pot, pour water over and boil gently. Strain and leave overnight to cool. Take the paste out and clean the pot. Mix in another 1½lb of *sampsuchum* and repeat the process: boil, strain. Store the unguent in a cool place. (Dioscorides II.92)

Theophrastus comments that the scent of sweet marjoram unguent was as durable as that of 'The Egyptian'.

Shaping unguent cakes(?). Wall-painting in Theban Tomb no. 175; 18th Dynasty.

Sampsuchinon was the name of a similarly scented oil made as follows:

Take thyme, cassia, southernwood, *sisymbrium* flowers [*Stachys germanica* or *Sisymbrium nastrurtium*], myrtle leaves, *sampsuchum*, as much of each as you consider will give a good balance. Beat the herbs together and pour over oil of unripe olives. Too much will overpower the fragrance of the herbs. Leave to macerate for four days, then strain. Repeat the process with fresh herbs. Choose the *sampsuchum* which is blackish green and with a sharp strong scent. This oil is warming and good for treatment of the vulva and pains in that region. But it is best used with honey. (Dioscorides 1.58)

There is yet another Egyptian ointment to be mentioned. Both Pliny (*NH*.xii.li) and Dioscorides (1.124) mention a tree called *cyprus*, of which the best quality grew at Canopus in the Delta. It has been identified as henna (*Lawsonia inermis* L.), which does indeed have fragrant flowers. Pliny provides the recipe:

Cyprinum

Take seeds of the *cyprus* tree and boil them in olive oil. Crush the seeds [and strain the oil].

Dioscorides adds that this ointment is sweet-smelling, heating and mollifying, and it mellows the taste of 'hot medicines' if taken with them.

Although some ancient unguents have been discovered in tombs, their present smell is by no means the original one, the fatty matter having been subject to chemical changes through the millennia. Some of the unguents found

54

Unguent vases as found in the tomb of Tutankhamun at Thebes. Egyptian Museum, Cairo.

The manufacture of unguents as represented in Theban Tomb no. 175; 18th Dynasty.

in the tomb of Tutankhamun, though still quite soft, had a rancid coconut-like smell which was not intended. The specimens examined contained about 90% animal fat and about 10% resin. Tutankhamun's unguent jars were all made of calcite (commonly known as 'alabaster'). This was for a good reason: Pliny explicitly says that unguents keep best in 'alabaster' containers (*NH*.XIII.iii). He adds that unguents improve with age, but he was probably not thinking in terms of thousands of years!

A fascinating glimpse of the processes involved in the preparation of unguents can be found in a scene from a wall-painting in a Theban tomb (no. 175), dated about 1400 BC. As there were no texts in the tomb we do not know who the owner was, but it would seem that he was in charge of the manufacture of unguents, perhaps for one of the temples in the area, or for the royal household. He is seated to the left in the picture, surveying the activities with a stick in his hand. The workers are grinding, boiling and sifting the ingredients which make up the fragrant end product.

Ladies with tall unguent cones. Fragment of wall-painting from a Theban tomb; 18th Dynasty. Römer-Pelizäus Museum, Hildesheim (1027).

56

With the above recipes in mind we can perhaps attempt to reconstruct a sequence of events in the representation, although it is just possible that individual stages of unrelated preparations are depicted. The words in square brackets describe activities which cannot be directly read from the picture.

1. Prepare chips of fragrant wood [and leave them to macerate in] wine.

2. Strain through a sieve.

3. Melt a quantity of fat in a vessel. Add sweet rush(?) [and the liquid from the wood chips]. Keep a [slow but] steady heat, and stir continuously. [Cool, and skim off the fat.]

4. Grind herbs and spices carefully.

5. Mix herbs and spices with the fat and shape to little cakes. [Leave covered overnight.]

6. Place the cakes in a broad pot. [Pour water over and] boil gently, stirring all the time.

7. [Leave to cool and skim off the scented fat.] Store in earthenware pots.

Another aromatic substance, used abundantly by Egyptian priests, was so important that the recipe was engraved on the walls of the temples and repeated in the works of the classical authors. A new study of the material is underway, but at present we must still rely on an article from 1887 (V. Loret, 'Le Kyphi'; see Bibliography). The famous *kyphi* was an oil- and fat-free scent, based on wine and raisins with a number of added aromatic herbs and resins. It was not used to perfume the body, but it was burnt in the temples. Loret had a pharmacist make up the three recipes given by Dioscorides, Plutarch and Galen respectively, and he came to the conclusion that the one quoted by Dioscorides was the most pleasant. In ancient times *kyphi* was also added to beverages. Loret informs us that the result was an acquired taste comparable to resinated wine. But in fumigation it was most agreeable:

Kyphi

Take ½ pint of *cyperus* [bulrush, 'thickening' agent] and ½ pint juniper berries; 12lb stoned plum raisins; 5lb resin; 1lb aromatic rush; 1lb *asphalatus* [see p. 52]; 1lb *iuncus odoratus* [*Cymbopogon schoenanthus*]; 1½oz myrrh; 8½ pint old wine; and 2lb honey. Stone and pound the raisins and grind with wine and myrrh. Pound and sift the other ingredients, except the honey, and mix with the raisins. Leave to steep for 1 day. Boil the honey until it thickens. Strain the raisin and herb mixture and blend with the honey. Store in an earthenware pot. (Dioscorides 1.24)

The hieroglyphic recipes are written on the walls of the temples of Edfu and Philae. Although some ingredients remain unidentified, they do not appear to be radically different from the classical versions. The recipe quoted below gives the essence of the ancient texts, largely based on Loret's interpretation.

Recipe for making 10,164g of excellent kyphi

1. Take 270g each of *Acorus calamus* L. [Sweet flag]; *Andropogon schoenanthus* L. [aromatic rush]; mastix; cassia; *tĭ-šps* [cinnamon?; for a new translation see pp. 88–9 below]; *ʿk3y* [mint?]; *db̯ʿ* [aspalathos?]; total 1870g. Grind and sieve. Only the powder is to be used, 2/5 of the total = 756g.

2. Take 270g each of juniper berries; an unidentified plant; *pkr*-plant; *Cyperus longus* L.; total 1080g. Grind. Add to this 2250g wine. Leave until the next morning. Half the wine will be absorbed by the herbs. The rest is to be discarded.

3. Take 1800g raisins and 2250g oasis wine. Grind together well. Remove the rind and pips of the raisins (weighing 1350g). Place the rest (weighing 2700g) in a pot with the herbs. Leave for five days.

4. Mix 1200g frankincense and 3000g honey in a vessel. Boil gently until thickened and reduced by 1/5, the total weight being 3360g. Mix with the other ingredients and leave for five days.

5. Add to this 1143g finely ground myrrh, and you will have 10,164g *kyphi*.

Medicine

The ingredients of pharaonic medical prescriptions were derived predominantly from plants and trees, and their fruit. A surprisingly large amount of those used have medicinal properties recognised in modern herbal medicine, and although the ancient physicians may not fully have understood why a particular plant was useful, they had certainly learnt from experience that the treatment was efficient.

Some remedies were taken, others were applied externally as poultices or in unguents, while in some cases fumigation or inhalation were prescribed. The latter was administered by means of a device consisting of a double pot. In one pot was placed a stone previously heated on the fire, over which the liquid herbal remedy was poured. The second pot was placed on top as a lid, but it had a hole pierced in the bottom through which a straw was inserted. The patient breathed through the straw and benefited to the full from the wholesome steam.

The individual ingredients of the prescriptions will be discussed in the Herbal below. The sources from which they derive are the medical papyri compiled during the latter half of the second millennium BC. These compilations were for the benefit of the men of the medical profession. The housewife would rely on experience and approximate measurements. When a remedy was prescribed by a doctor, it sometimes came in a container with the prescription written on it, very much like our labelled bottles. For instance, one Egyptian suffering from an eye complaint was given a small cylindrical pottery vase which specified the contents and gave instructions as to their application: 'sawdust; acacia leaves; zinc oxide [or oxide of manganese?]; goose fat. Apply as a bandage'.

In order to avoid the frustration of a large number of herbs which have not yet been identified with any certainty, only prescriptions with few or no unidentified substances have been given. It is thus by no means a corpus of herbal medicine that is presented, but a variety of prescriptions, the translations of which are reasonably certain and which can be analysed and perhaps tried out.

Some Coptic remedies have been included. Coptic is a late form of the ancient Egyptian language, but written in Greek letters with a few Egyptian signs added. This was the language of the earliest Christians in Egypt from the second to the seventh century AD, until Arabic gradually took over, and it is still used in the Coptic liturgy. The prescriptions were used among the monks and in the Christian community towards the end of the first millennium AD. In general, Coptic medicine is not held in very high esteem, and the pharmacopoeia includes many ingredients which do not appear to have been used in pharaonic times. But although Coptic medicine relied heavily on Greek and Arab sources, the conventional use of some remedies never went out of fashion, and some may still be in use among the peasants as they were just a hundred years ago.

Nebamun, an Egyptian physician, administering to a Syrian client. Wall-painting in Theban Tomb no. 17; 18th Dynasty.

The Herbal

The following pages present a selection of the plant material available to the ancient Egyptians, from herbs to trees, native and imported. The criteria for inclusion are as varied as the sources themselves. The actual remains of a plant, found in an excavation, are usually not considered sufficient on their own, but they must be supported by some indication of the use of the plant either – ideally – in the ancient Egyptian texts; in texts from contemporary neighbouring civilisations; in treatises by classical authors; or in the medical works of the Copts.

An essential problem in translating and using the ancient herbal prescriptions lies in identifying the various ingredients listed. The hieroglyphic script uses a way of writing the words which makes it easier to determine the category of word intended: a name of a plant concludes with a miniature drawing of a plant; a wooden object has a branch, and so on. But to distinguish individual plants is a field of research where a considerable amount of work remains to be done. One of the clues is the Coptic equivalent of the word, based on the ancient Egyptian, but written in Greek characters. When the Arabs conquered Egypt, they soon felt the need of a Coptic–Arabic vocabulary. Among others they compiled a 'scala', as it was called, of plant names listing the Coptic and Arabic nomenclature. As the Arabic names are often known from other sources, and some are still in use, the 'scala' is most helpful in identifying Coptic plant names and, tracing them further back, the ancient Egyptian equivalents. But the matter is complicated by the fact that the Copts often borrowed names from Greek, and any link to an older Egyptian name would thus be lost. The problems and possibilities of identifying plants are discussed further below (pp. 159–62).

In many cases all these sources can be consulted for one plant, for the tradition of herbal medicine is firmly rooted. For this reason we have also, where appropriate, made reference to traditional Islamic medicine and to the acute observations by Prospero Alpini, a Venetian physician who sojourned in Egypt in 1581–4 and whose important works have recently been translated into French (Alpin, *Médicine*, & Alpin, *Plantes*). A survey of the use of herbs in Cairo in more recent times and published in 1930 has also been taken into account (Ducros, *Essai sur le droguier populaire arabe . . .*).

A full bibliography will be found at the end of the book, but for quick reference the abbreviations and the date of the sources are listed here.

Ancient Egyptian texts:

Bln = P. Berlin 3038 (1300 BC)

B = P. Chester Beatty VI (1300 BC)

E = P. Ebers (1550 BC)

H = P. Hearst (1550 BC)

Sm = P. Edwin Smith (1500 BC)

Ram III = P. Ramesseum III (1700 BC)

Ram V = P. Ramesseum V (1700 BC)

Coptic texts:

BA = pp. 214–15 of an otherwise lost book on medicine

BKU 1–9 = page of a parchment manuscript

BKU 14–5 = ostracon

Ch = P. Chassinat

MK = sheet of paper with two prescriptions

Ryl = fragments of paper with medical prescriptions

WM = pp. 167–8 of an otherwise lost work, translated from Greek

TM = a page of paper with medical prescriptions

ZB = pp. 241–4 of an otherwise lost book on medicine

Ch has been dated to the ninth century AD. The others are probably contemporary copies of older works.

Classical sources:

Apicius 1st century AD

Athenaeus 3rd century AD

Diodorus 1st century BC

Dioscorides 1st century AD

Herodotus *c.*484–420 BC

Pliny 23–79 AD

Theophrastus *c.*372–*c.*287 BC

Xenophon *c.*430–*c.*355 BC

The work quoted as the Assyrian Herbal is a compilation of vegetable drugs undertaken by R. Campbell Thompson in 1924 based on the material available at the time, among others 128 fragments of cuneiform plant lists and 660 tablets with medical texts, dating to the end of the second millennium and the first millennium BC. Reference has also been made to some Sumerian texts from the third and second millennia.

Weights and measures

Apothecaries are often concerned with minute quantities of many ingredients. The pharaonic prescriptions use a unit of *ro* and fractions of another measure of capacity, about which there has been some discussion. The two units suggested are: a) a unit of 5 *ro*, which was then subdivided; or b) a unit of a so-called *dja*, more than four times larger than 5 *ro*. The latter is the most realistic since the quantities would otherwise be ridiculously small. The following conversion table may be useful:

unit of *dja*	1	½	1/4	1/8	1/16	1/32	1/64
	320ml	160ml	80ml	40ml	20ml	10ml	5ml

When '1' is prescribed either '1 *ro*' is meant, or it can be taken simply as '1 part'. For larger quantities of liquid a *hin* was sometimes preferred: 1 *hin* = 32 *ro* = 480ml

The Copts weighed their ingredients and indicated the quantities in *obolos* and *drachme*: 1 obolos = *c.*0.75g; 1 drachme = *c.*3.75g.

Ancient Egyptian ⸗ ◌ ⸗ *ˁš*; the oil probably ⸗ ◌ *sft*

Coptic ?

Greek πεύϰη

Modern Egyptian Arabic تنوب اناطولي *tannûb anatôli* or شوح *šôḥ*

The source for fir timber and fir resin was Syria and Asia Minor. Fir trees still grow in Lebanon. They were imported into Egypt from an early date, and fir resin has been found in Old Kingdom tombs. A small calcite jar in the tomb of Tutankhamun was labelled 'fir resin', and it still contained a small amount. The timber was used for carpentry, and the resin in mummification and in medicine. Both oil and resin are antiseptic, diuretic and carminative.

A vaginal suppository made of fir resin, juniper and an unidentified plant was used to help birth (E 806). A remedy to soften stiff limbs consisted of:

natron 1; Lower Egyptian salt 1; fir resin 1; dregs of sweet beer; to be applied as a bandage. (E 690)

The beneficial properties of the oil were extracted from the wood by steeping the chips in a liquid which has been identified as fermented plant juice:

Cutting fir trees in Syria. Relief on the external wall of the hypostyle hall of the temple of Amun at Karnak; 19th Dynasty.

A remedy to treat swelling: fir wood; chop it in fermented plant juice with the broken bottom of a new [i.e. clean] pot. Use as a bandage. (E 574)

Fir oil manufactured from the resin has been identified with some certainty as the *sft* of the medical texts. It was used as a worm expellant with red natron and an unidentified fruit (E 77), and as a face wash with honey and an unidentified ingredient. Made into a dough and mixed with fermented plant juice it was used to treat wrinkles (E 719). A polluted wound was kept clean and made to open with a bandage of ibex fat, fir oil, and crushed peas (E 522b), a remedy that would have proved efficient because of the antiseptic properties of the oil.

Fir lotion to promote hair growth has been quoted above (see section on Cosmetics).

Acacia nilotica Desf. Acacia

Ancient Egyptian 𓇓𓈖𓆓𓏏 *šndt*

Coptic: tree ϢⲞⲚⲦⲈ; juice ⲁⲕⲁⲕⲓⲁ

Greek ἀκακία

Modern Egyptian Arabic: tree سنط *sant*; pod juice اقاقية *âqâqîya*

The acacia is a tall tree with dark stems and branches and bright yellow flowers.

An unusual bouquet including acacia branches(?). Wall-painting in Theban Tomb no. 19 after a drawing by Hay; Ramesside. British Library (Hay MSS 29851, 167).

The pods with their characteristic indentations are up to 15cm long and contain 30% tannin. The tree grows abundantly in Egypt today.

Among the classical authors Theophrastus mentions that the Egyptians used acacia for tanning (IV.2.1 and 8). Pliny, who copied extensively from Theophrastus in his works, adds that the best gum was that of the Egyptian acacia (*NH*.XIII.xx).

In pharaonic times the wood was used for timber, the bark for tanning and the leaves, flowers and pods found multiple use in medicine. It was taken internally for a number of ailments:

A remedy to kill worm: leaves of acacia are placed in a jar with water and left overnight covered with cloth. Rise early in the morning and grind it in a stone mortar until it has been reduced to a paste. Rub a rush to the nose of the patient when he has drunk it. (E 68)

The last phrase is cryptic. Perhaps the patient was supposed to sneeze?

Another remedy to kill worm: acacia leaves 5 ro; water 10 ro; remains overnight in the dew, is strained and then taken for one day. (E 52)

A remedy for cough: acacia leaves; honey; sweet beer; is drunk by the patient. (Bln 40)

Acacia tree. Wall-painting in a Theban Tomb no. 31; Ramesside.

The astringent effect of acacia leaves was utilised in external applications:

A remedy for swollen legs: acacia leaves; zizyphus leaves; ochre; honey; is applied as a poultice. (Bln 131)

A remedy for the toes: ox fat; acacia leaves; boil to a paste and apply. (H 180)

A remedy to cool the vessels and make stiff what is weak: fresh acacia leaves 1; ox fat 1; sawdust of fir 1; grind together and use as a bandage for four days. (Ram v No. XIII)

A remedy to soothe the bone when it is broken: acacia leaves 1; gum 1; water 1; is combined and used as a bandage for four days. (H 223)

A remedy to heal a wound: acacia leaves 1; are pounded, mixed with oil or fat and applied to the wound. (E 527)

A remedy to stop the blood which has been taken to the heart and has spread: dried acacia leaves; are ground and mixed with oil or fat. Heat to finger warmth and use as a bandage. (Bln 151)

The Copts found use for gum, twigs, leaves and flowers of acacia. Acacia was part of preparations for the eyes:

An eye remedy: opium; acacia leaves; acacia juice; copper; gum; grind equal quantities of each, make it into an eye ointment and apply externally. (Ch 50)

A remedy for pains in the eye and head: opium; acacia leaves; is ground and kneaded with water and applied. It will heal. (Ch 86)

The credit for the efficacy of these two remedies is undoubtedly due more to the opium than to the acacia leaves. These latter were included in a remedy to be taken:

A remedy for someone who spits blood out of his mouth: acacia leaves 2 drachma; pomegranate rind 1 drachme; hazelnut 1 obolos; chicory 2 drachma; wild fennel 1 drachme; flowers of safflower 6 drachma; is ground well, kneaded with honey and the patient made to eat as much as he can. (Ch 233)

Acacia flowers mixed with eggwhite were used as a mask for people suffering from the skin disease called *psora* (Ch 61).

An acacia concentrate was prepared by steeping leaves(?) in water, placing the pot in the oven until it boiled, leaving it in the sun and stirring it (BKU 14–5). The resulting liquid entered preparations for eye complaints, and as a treatment for the uterus: equal measures of an unidentified ingredient called *triatos* and *akakia* were steeped in oil for three days, then applied internally with a tampon (Ch 123).

Prospero Alpini says that the Egyptians of his time used an enema for diarrhoea consisting of a decoction of the leaves, unripe fruits and flowers (*Médicine*, 314).

Acorus calamus L.   Sweet flag

Ancient Egyptian 𓄿𓇌𓈖𓏤 *ḳnỉ*

Coptic ?

Greek ἄκορον; κάλαμος ἀρωματικός; κάλαμος ὁ εὔωδης

Modern Egyptian Arabic وج *wag*; rhizome قصب الذريرة *qaṣab el-zorîra*

Sweet flag is an aromatic perennial with rhizome 3cm thick, sword-shaped leaves and small flowers. It grows by water. The dried rhizome is today used as a vermifuge and carminative, and also to flavour beer and liquor. In a powdered state it is ant repellant; it fixes perfume, and it can be used as tooth powder and dry hair shampoo. In Egypt it is considered to have aphrodisiac properties.

The extent to which the plant was used for any of these purposes in ancient Egypt remains uncertain, but it was certainly known and used for perfuming oil (cf. Dioscorides I.17). It occurs rarely in the medical texts, but in one source it is one of several ingredients used in a bandage to treat a stomach ailment (B 10). Interestingly, in traditional Islamic medicine it is also considered good for inflammation of the stomach and liver, and applied in a bandage it is said to have cured a pustule on the finger of the Prophet. Burns would be treated with a mixture of sweet flag, rose oil and vinegar.

Alkanna tinctoria Tausch.   Alkanet

Ancient Egyptian 𓈖𓊪𓏥 *nstỉ*

Coptic ?

Greek ?

Modern Egyptian Arabic رجل الحمامة *rigl el-ḥammâma* ('pigeon's leg') or شجرة الدم *šagaret ed-damm* ('blood tree')

Alkanet is a plant about 30cm high. It has a thick root with purplish root bark. It grows in Egypt today, as it did in the first centuries AD. A papyrus found at Thebes, but written in Greek, mentions alkanet as a source for red dye. Even today this is the principal use of the herb and its roots. With oil or alcohol as a mordant it yields a red dye, whereas with the addition of alum the colour becomes grey-green. Today it is used to colour cloth and rouge. It is also employed as an antiseptic ointment.

In pharaonic medicine it was used for a similar purpose. An unguent to treat inflammation consisted of powdered carob pod, powdered beans, alkanet, a resin, moringa oil and 'pure oil' (E 107). Alkanet is furthermore reported to have been used to colour the candles which lit the temple of Edfu in Upper Egypt.

Theophrastus mentions alkanet for dyeing perfume red (*Concerning Odours* VI.31).

Allium cepa L.   Onion

Ancient Egyptian 𓏏𓄿𓏲 *ḥḏw*

Coptic ⲘⲬⲰⲗ

Greek κρόμυον

Modern Egyptian Arabic بصل *baṣal*

Onions grow all over the world and are a major crop in Egyptian agriculture. Onion juice is antibiotic, diuretic and expectorant, and is used in herbal medicine to treat coughs, colds and stomach ailments. It is rubbed on cuts and acne. The bulbs are used for human consumption and flavouring, as they were in ancient Egypt.

In the classical world onion juice was used to treat the ears. In pharaonic medicine it was prescribed for other complaints:

To stop a woman from menstruating: onions 1; wine 1; is made into a paste and placed in her vagina. (E 828)

To prevent 'blood eating' in any limb: onions are ground in fat and applied. (E 724)

Onions found use in mummification, one or two being placed in the thorax or pelvis, or in the ear or near the eyes. The use of an onion as a snake repellant has been quoted above.

'Doing the onions'.
Relief from a tomb at
Memphis; 5th Dynasty.
Ägyptisches Museum,
West Berlin (Inv. nr.
3/65).

Allium kurrat Schweinf. ex Krause or *Allium porrum* L.   Leek

Ancient Egyptian 𓇋𓃀𓈖𓏏𓏦 *i3ḳt*

Coptic ⲎⲈⲈ

Greek πράςον

Modern Egyptian Arabic كرات رومي *kurrât rûmi*

Like onions, leeks were used for human consumption as well as in medicine, though they were much less frequent.

A remedy to cool the vessels in all limbs: zizyphus leaves 1; willow leaves 1; acacia leaves 1; Lower Egyptian salt 1; leek 'fruits'; is ground finely and applied as a bandage for four days. (H 238)

In Coptic medicine they were used in prescriptions for the eyes:

For a man who cannot see at night: leek and fresh urine. Fill his eyes frequently with it, so that he will get to see well. (Ch 201)

There is an interesting parallel to the use of urine as a cure for blindness in a story of an Egyptian prince of about 1000 BC. Only urine from a woman who had never deceived her husband would do, and it took a considerable length of time until the prince was cured (Herodotus II.111). The Copts used leeks in a treatment for warts on the private parts:

kohl and dry leek; grind it together, knead it with honey and apply. (Ch 141)

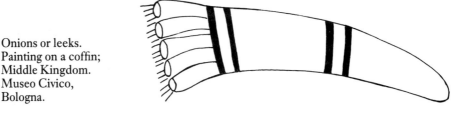

Onions or leeks.
Painting on a coffin;
Middle Kingdom.
Museo Civico,
Bologna.

Allium sativum L.   Garlic

Ancient Egyptian 𓏺𓃀𓏏𓈖𓏦 *ḥtn*

Coptic ⲱϪⲎⲚ

Greek σκόρδον

Modern Egyptian Arabic توم *tôm*

Garlic is native to Asia. Its characteristic taste is much favoured in warmer climates. In medicine it is used as an antibacterial and for catarrh and colds.

The ancient name for garlic as quoted above is strangely absent from pharaonic medical texts. In Akkadian it was known as *šûmu*, a word closely related to the Arabic. In view of the tradition for garlic in medicine we shall perhaps have to look for the item under a different designation. The word *ḫtn* is a likely candidate because of its similarity with Babylonian *ha-za-nu*, but this word only occurs in an offering list. For a medical context the word *t3 n ḥḏw* has been suggested, *ḥḏw* meaning 'white' (cf. Danish 'hvidløg' = 'white onion').

Cloves of garlic have been discovered in Egyptian burials, including the tomb of Tutankhamun, and in the sacred animal temple precinct at Saqqâra. Pliny devotes a lengthy section to the praises of garlic: it kept off serpents and scorpions by its smell; mixed with honey, it was used as an ointment for dog bites, and serpents' bites and bruises were treated with roasted garlic in oil. Raw garlic was given to asthmatics; fresh garlic and coriander in wine was a purgative and an aphrodisiac. Pounded in vinegar and water, it was used as a gargle for quinsy and toothache. Garlic juice and goose grease made good eardrops. In soft cheese, or a gruel of peas or beans, it relieved hoarseness. Garlic pounded in salt and vinegar was used to treat bruises. Finally, it was thought to induce sleep (*NH*.xx.xxiii).

In Coptic medicine garlic is prescribed mixed with oil for a skin disease called *psora* (zb 22), and it was believed to stimulate the production of milk in women:

Take dried garlic; boil it in wine. The patient is to drink of it for three days in the bath. (BA 6)

The Copts also prescribed a complete 'garlic cure'. They recommended garlic eaten first thing in the morning. During the day one was to abstain from eating fish, vegetables and milk (and also from being with a woman). Instead a cooked dish was suggested consisting of more garlic, pomegranate, raisins, vinegar, honey and a selection of herbs and spices. This diet was believed to cleanse the intestines and clear the head (Ryl 4).

Garlic was widely consumed by the Egyptians. Herodotus has the following to say: 'There is an inscription of Egyptian characters on the pyramid which records the quantities of radishes, onions and garlic consumed by the labourers who constructed it' (II.125). The pyramid builders undoubtedly consumed large quantities of garlic and certainly of ordinary onions. But the source of Herodotus' information remains cryptic, since no pyramids bore any inscriptions relating to the affairs of mortal men. For the 'radishes' see below.

Ancient Egyptian 𓄿𓏏𓂝𓅓𓏭 *ḫt-ʿw3*
Coptic: juice ⲁⲗⲱⲏ
Greek: juice ἀλόη
Modern Egyptian Arabic صبر *sabir*

Aloe is a succulent plant with clusters of fleshy leaves, prickly at the margin and the tip. It may produce a woody stem up to 15m tall. It carries spikes of yellow, orange and red flowers. It is a native of south and east Africa. The juice contains volatile oil and aloins which are purgative. It is nowadays used as a soothing and moisturing ingredient in skin care products, and to heal skin inflammation, sores and burns. Because of its purgative effect, it is contraindicated for pregnancy and haemorrhoids.

The use of aloe can be traced. Prospero Alpini relates that Egyptian women of his day perfumed their private parts with it (*Médicine*, 230), and that the wood was used in composite remedies to treat fever and plague (*Médicine*, 318, 320, 323). Aloe was known to the Greeks, for Alexander is said to have been instructed to conquer the island of Socotra between Somalia and Hadramout where the plants grew. In the Bible the plant was known as *ahaloth* and it was used as a perfuming agent (e.g. John 19:39–40). The Assyrian Herbal prescribes *sibaru* for the stomach and difficult breathing (§ 10 CD 2).

In the ancient Egyptian medical texts *ḫt-ʿw3* has been suggested for aloe, and its use here reflects the Assyrian prescription:

To expel catarrh in the nose: stibium; aloe; dry myrrh; honey: [it] is anointed therewith for four days. Make [it] and you shall see, behold it is a true remedy. (E 63)

One of the plants represented in Egyptian art so frequently that it is nearly stereotyped could be the aloe. It is used to suggest a desert environment, as for example on a painted shrine of Tutankhamun. Only the leaves are shown.

The Copts used aloe with other ingredients to treat eye diseases, swellings and digestive disorders. The skin disease called *psora* was treated with an unguent based on aloe:

If you take a baked cucumber and grind it with aloe, add wine and anoint the affected parts with it, they will heal. (ZB 10)

Desert plant, possibly aloe. From the painted box of
Tutankhamun. Egyptian Museum, Cairo.

Ancient Egyptian ?

Coptic ⲘⲞⲖⲞⲬⲎ ⲚⲀⲄⲢⲒⲀ

Greek ἀλθαία (= μαλαχη ἡ ἀγρια)

Modern Egyptian Arabic خطمية *ḥiṭmiya*

Marshmallow is an erect perennial, growing to 1.25m, with hairy leaves and stem, and white or pink flowers with five petals. It grows wild in Europe and Asia. It was not native to Egypt, but was introduced from Syria. It is a soothing, healing herb, and it is frequently used in medicine, a decoction of the root having been prescribed for asthma, bronchitis, hoarseness (the famous althaea sweets), and to relieve inflammations and gastritis. The flowers, leaves and seeds are used in infusions. *Althaea officinalis* is the variety most frequently used in modern times. Theophrastus mentions its roots mixed in sweet wine for coughs (XVIII.1).

   Althaea ficifolia has been identified in the garlands adorning the mummies of kings Amosis and Amenophis I, being set alternately with willow leaves, *Delphinium orientale*, acacia flowers, lotus petals and flowers of *Sesbania aegyptiaca*.

   When writing of the plant Dioscorides said that the Egyptians called it *khokorten* (III.163), but there may here be some confusion with *Malva*, a herb with similar properties. Another Greek name was οὐρα μυός ('mouse tail'), and this may possibly be a literal translation of 𓂋𓅓𓏏𓏛 *sd pnw* 'mouse tail' which occurs once in the Egyptian medical texts:

A remedy to cool the anus: powdered colocynth 1/32; 'mouse tail' 1/32; honey 1/4; water 5 ro; is strained and drunk for four days. (E 160)

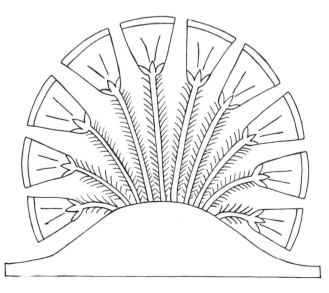

Pink flowers, possibly *Althaea*, copied by Rosellini from a wall-painting.

The use of the plant is reflected in a prescription in a Coptic text mentioning what is probably *Althaea ficifolia*:

A treatment for the anus: vitriol of copper; onion leaves; roasted euphorbia [dried juice of the stem of *Euphorbia resinifera* Berg.]; leaves of marshmallow. Pound it together with oil of roses. Apply with an ibis feather. But first claim the fee. (Ch 212)

Anethum graveolens L.   Dill

Ancient Egyptian ⌇ *imst*

Coptic ⲁⲙⲓⲥⲓ

Greek ἄνηθον

Modern Egyptian Arabic شبت *šabat*

Dill is an umbelliferous annual with feathery aromatic leaves and umbels with yellow flowers. Dill leaves and, to some extent, dill seeds are widely used in cooking, particularly in Scandinavian countries, where it accompanies shellfish, and the unripe flower head is an important flavouring agent in pickled gherkins. In herbal medicine dill seeds are considered sedative, soothing and digesting, relieving flatulence, colicky pains in babies and even hiccups. In Egyptian gardens today it is grown particularly because of its fragrant leaves, used in cooking.

Dioscorides says that it was called *arakhou* in Egyptian (III.67), but its name has been identified as quoted above. In ancient Egypt dill was an ingredient in a pain-killing mixture:

A remedy for killing pains in all parts of the body: dill 1/32; dates 1/8; raisins 1/8; wine 5 ro; is boiled, strained and drunk for four days. (H 44)

The seeds were used in an unguent for headache along with bryony, coriander, donkey's fat and two unidentified plants (E 249), and in a poultice for the 'vessels' of the shoulder including myrrh, frankincense, chaste-tree, grass, sawdust of fir, sycamore figs, fermented plant juice and three unidentified items (E 658). For the 'vessels' of the neck, a poultice was applied for four days mixed from 'water from the laundry-man', honey, dill, and part of an unidentified tree (Bln 163e).

The Copts used dill as a mouth rinse:

A sick mouth: alum 1 drachme; dill 1 drachme; God knows that this remedy is a good one! (Ch 157)

Dill stems with leaves and flowers were found on the mummy of Amenophis II.

Anthemis tinctoria L.   Dyer's camomile

Ancient Egyptian ?

Coptic ⲭⲁⲙⲉⲙⲉⲗⲟⲛ ?

Greek ἄνθεμον

Modern Egyptian Arabic بابونج أصفر *bâbûnag asfar* ('yellow camomile') or عين التور ʿ*ên it-tôr* ('ox eye')

This variety of camomile has yellow flowers and yields a strong dye. With chrome as a mordant it gives a tawny orange, with iron a greenish-brown colour. Its use in dyeing in ancient Egypt has not yet been established, but it was used for this purpose in Assyria (in Akkadian called *qurban egli*, 'gift of the field'). One of the floral collars found in the tomb of Tutankhamun contained these yellow flowers. Powdered remains of *Anthemidae* Sp. were sprinkled into the abdominal cavity of Ramesscs II, probably as an insecticide.

    Unlike the well-known white camomile (*Chamemelum nobile*), dyer's camomile is not generally used for medicinal purposes. The Assyrian Herbal however, recommends it for application to the anus 'when it makes a pustule' (§ 10 x). The Egyptian word must be among the unidentified plant names of the medical texts.

Anthriscus cerefolium (L.) Hoffm.   Chervil

Ancient Egyptian ?

Coptic ?

Greek ?

Modern Egyptian Arabic (probably) بقدونس افرنجي *baqdûnis afrangi* ('French parsley')

The umbelliferous chervil is native to the Middle East. In France it is a much-favoured culinary herb, and in Scandinavia a soup is made from it. In medicine it is taken internally to cleanse the blood, or it is applied as a soothing poultice and as skin lotion.

    Evidence of the herb in Egypt is scarce, but it certainly was part of the ancient flora, for a basket of its seeds was included in the burial equipment of Tutankhamun.

Ancient Egyptian ⳤⳤ *m3tt*

Coptic ΜΙΤ

Greek σέλινον

Modern Egyptian Arabic كرفس *karafs*

Celery is a biennial plant with bulbous, fleshy root and strong-smelling leaves. It grows wild in Africa, Europe and the Americas. It is a tonic, an appetiser and carminative. The fresh juice is diuretic. It was once used as a slimming herb. Celery grows in Egyptian gardens today as it did in pharaonic times, at least towards the end of the New Kingdom (*c.* 1000 BC). Garlands have been found on mummies from this period, where celery leaves alternated with petals of *Nymphaea caerulea*.

The plant is frequently mentioned in Egyptian texts. Dioscorides gave the Egyptian name as *mith* (III.75), which through Coptic has been identified with ancient Egyptian *m3tt*. This is easily confused with the name for parsley, which is called 'mountain celery' (see under *Apium petroselinum* L.). In a few instances seeds or fruits of celery are specified, but most often no particular part of the plant is indicated. Celery was used to treat a variety of diseases:

A remedy to stimulate the appetite: fat meat 1/16; wine 5 ro; raisins 1/16; figs 1/16; celery 1/16; sweet beer 25 ro; is boiled, strained and drunk for four days. (E 291)

A remedy to treat the teeth and fix them consisted of celery, sweet beer, and an unidentified plant, chewed and spat out (E 748). Celery was used to cure a disease cast by a demon, once with an unidentified plant and beer (E 236). Twice it is recommended for gynaecological purposes:

A remedy to cool the uterus: frankincense; celery; is ground finely in cow's milk; strain through a cloth and administer to the vagina. (E 822)

It is used as a contraceptive after fumigation with emmer seeds:

Oil or fat 5 ro; celery 5 ro; sweet beer 5 ro; is boiled and taken for four mornings. (Bln 192)

It is interesting in this context that a large dose of the related *Apium petroselinum* L. was once thought to be capable of causing abortion. Prospero Alpini mentions that a decoction of celery seeds was used to warm the stomach of women who had not had their periods (*Médicine,* 315).

'Celery from the Delta' was crushed and applied as a bandage to darken a burn (E 502), or celery, fir resin, fir oil and an unidentified plant were mixed and applied, a remedy proven good for burns 'in the days of the King of Upper and Lower Egypt, Amenophis III' (E 487 = L 51).

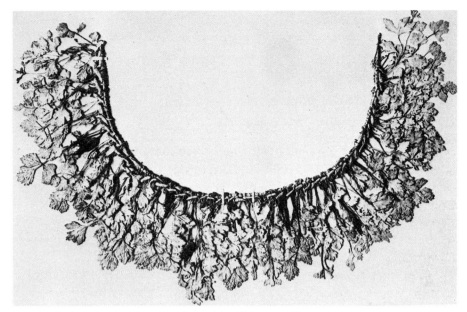

A garland of celery; 20th Dynasty. Agricultural Museum, Cairo.

A remedy to treat a 'nest' of blood which has not yet settled: ox fat 1; frankincense 1; cyperus grass from the garden 1; cyperus grass from the river land 1; sawdust of fir 1; costly unguent 1; dry myrrh 1; resin 1; celery 1; is pounded to a paste and used as a poultice. (E 594)

A remedy to stop blood in the eye: frankincense 1; celery 1; place it in both eyes. (E 352)

A similar eye remedy included hemp (cf. below under *Cannabis*).

A remedy to treat the tongue: *kohl* 1; celery 1; ochre 1; copper slags 1; chew it and spit it out. (E 700).

A remedy for the temples: celery is pounded in cold water and placed on the temples of the patient so that he gets well soon. (E 363)

A remedy for swollen limbs: celery ground in oil or fat. Anoint the vessels herewith. (H 113)

A Coptic remedy including MIT was prescribed for a painful stomach, along with roasted cumin. It was ground with eggwhite and applied (Ch 71).

Apium petroselinum L.   Parsley

Ancient Egyptian ⟨𓄿⟩ *m3tt ḥ3st* ('mountain celery')?

Coptic ⲗⲁⲧ or ⲥⲉⲗⲓⲛⲏ

Greek σέλινον; ὀρεοσέλινον ('mountain celery')

Modern Egyptian Arabic بقدونس *baqdûnis*

Parsley grows wild in southern Europe, and is now cultivated in gardens in most countries. The essential oil stimulates the appetite and regulates menstruation, but its main use now is that of a culinary herb.

Parsley is probably what is called in the Egyptian texts 'mountain celery'. It occurs in a few medical prescriptions for pain in the stomach or, in one instance, to 'contract the urine', where it is mixed with Lower Egyptian celery, juniper berries, porridge and five other ingredients (E 282). This particular use of parsley is interesting, since in modern herbal medicine parsley is considered diuretic.

Aristolochia clematitis L.   Birthwort

Ancient Egyptian ?

Coptic ?

Greek ἀριστολόχεια

Arabic زراوند *zarâwind*

Birthwort is a perennial with an erect or slightly twining stem growing to 50cm. It has heart-shaped dark green leaves with long petioles and yellowish-green flowers. It grows wild in Europe, North America and Japan. The long root is used dried, the rest of the plant fresh as a diaphoretic, emmenagogue and stimulant. The juice from the stems was once used to induce childbirth.

It is exactly this latter use which makes it relevant for ancient Egypt, for a plant which has obvious similarities with *Aristolochia* is almost invariably shown in scenes connected with childbirth. Although Dioscorides says that the Egyptians called the plant *soboeph* (III.6), the word has not been identified in the ancient texts. But Theophrastus provides us with detailed information of its use in his days: it was used for sores on the head; bites of reptiles; to induce sleep; for disorders of the womb. It was either steeped in water and then used as a plaster; or it was taken shredded in honey and olive oil. To induce sleep it was 'scraped up' and taken in dry red wine. To treat prolapsus uteri it was made into a lotion with water and applied, at times as a pessary (IX.13.2 and IX.20.4).

It would seem that Theophrastus includes the use of *Aristolochia serpentaria*

(*Above left*) An intimate scene on an ostracon from the village of Deir el-Medîna (Thebes), showing the characteristic climbing plant, possibly *Aristolochia*. British Museum (8506).

(*Above right*) A floral garland and a trailing plant. The identification of this plant has proved problematic: some representations may depict *Aristolochia*. Wall-painting in Theban Tomb no. 217; Ramesside.

L., snakeroot, in his comments. This plant has an erect stem growing to 40cm bearing heart-shaped pointed leaves and purple to brown flowers. Its dried root is tonic, and diaphoretic; it was once used to treat snake bites and infectious diseases. There is no direct evidence for this herb in ancient Egypt, but this may be a coincidence. Prospero Alpini mentions both, but says that it was the 'round' one, meaning presumably *Aristolochia rotunda*, which was used to treat scorpion bites, mixed with caper root in aromatic wine (*Médicine*, 310); the 'long' variety (presumably *Aristolochia serpentaria*, which has longer leaves) was used to treat children with smallpox: it was ground to a powder with several other ingredients and taken to promote perspiration (*Médicine*, 321).

For the identification of this particular plant, see pp. 160–2.

Ancient Egyptian ⌐⌐𓏤𓆼𓏤 *s'm*

Coptic ?

Greek ἀψίνθιον

Modern Egyptian Arabic افسنتين *afsantîn*

Wormwood is a perennial shrub which grows in warm places, preferably near the sea. It has a hairy stem and aromatic leaves covered in down. The flowers have minute, yellow florets. It grows wild in central Europe, North America and Asia, and has also been introduced into gardens. The bitter leaves are used to flavour vermouth and absinth. They contain santonin, which in overdoses causes vertigo and delirium. It also aids digestion, stimulates the appetite and is antiseptic.

Among the classical authors Theophrastus noted that, although it was a bitter herb, it was also wholesome (VII.5.5). Dioscorides quotes it as being used to expel intestinal worms (III.26), a practice already known in pharaonic Egypt:

A remedy to expel worm: leaves of pondweed 5 ro; wormwood 5 ro; sweet beer 20 ro; is ground together, strained and drunk. (E 56)

Another: melilot 1; wormwood 1; fermented plant juice 1; is mixed and eaten. The patient will expel all the worms which are in his belly. (E 64)

A pain in the anus of demonic origin was treated with:

wormwood 1/8; juniper berries 1/16; honey 1/32; sweet beer 10 ro; is strained and drunk for four days. (E 138)

An inflammation of the skin was thought to be cured by letting the patient drink a mixture of bryony root, wormwood, dried dates and an unidentified fruit, which caused vomiting (Bln 108), and a cough was eased with a mixture of wormwood, peas, fermented plant juice and an unidentified ingredient (Bln 32). Another treatment was to let the patient inhale through a straw a mixture of alum, wormwood and an unidentified ingredient (Bln 46). A strengthening and soothing unguent consisted of:

serpent's fat 1; wormwood 1; *kohl* 1; is combined and applied with myrrh. (H 98)

Prospero Alpini quotes a decoction of *Artemisia* to expel a bilious fever and used with other herbs in hot oil for a light massage to bring out excess body heat before an attack of contagious fever (*Médicine*, 315).

Balanites aegyptiaca L. Balanos

Ancient Egyptian ?

Coptic ?

Greek βάλανος

Modern Egyptian Arabic هجليج *heglîg*

This fiercely thorny tree was once very abundant in the Nile Valley, but is now rare. The fruit looks like a date with a brittle shell, including a mass with a hard kernel. The oil derived from it is slightly yellow.

The classical authors mention balanos as part of the famous Mendesian unguent. Theophrastus mentions that the Egyptian perfumers used the husks of the fruit which they bruised (IV.2.6). The fruit is indeed frequent among archaeological finds, but as long as its ancient name has not been established beyond doubt, its use remains somewhat obscure.

Bryonia dioica Jacq. White bryony

Ancient Egyptian 𓈖𓂝𓅓𓏭𓏤𓏛 *ḫ3syt*

Coptic ?

Greek ?

Modern Egyptian Arabic (*Bryonica cretica* L.) عنب الحية ʿ*inab el- ḥaya* ('grapes of life')

This vigorous perennial herb with five-lobed rough leaves grows wild in the Mediterranean. Male plants have pale-green flowers on long stalks, whereas female plants bear greenish flowers on short stalks and single red berries. It is not to be confused with Black bryony, *Tamus communis* L., although in Arabic medicine the two are often juxtaposed. The plant contains bryonin, tannin and volatile oil. Although it is highly poisonous, it has been used as a purgative and to relieve headache. *A Compleat English Dispensatory* from 1749 prescribed Bryony Water as a uterine detergent.

In ancient Egypt bryony was taken internally, but it was stated in one prescription that the treatment was not to be repeated. Some varieties of bryony are still to be found in Egypt. The herb was used to treat bladder disorders:

A remedy to treat urination: rush 1/8; dates 1/4; tips(?) of bryony 1/4; honey 2½ ro; juniper berries 1/4; water 20 ro; is strained and drunk for four days. (E 263)

Another prescription is for the treatment of the stomach:

A remedy for a swollen belly: figs 1/8; persea fruit(?) 1/8; raisins 1/8; notched sycamore fruits 1/8; berries of bryony 1/8; ochre 1/32; frankincense 1/64; water. To be exposed to the dew overnight and drunk for four days. (E 39)

A digestive ailment was successfully treated with a remedy including bryony:

To cool the anus: grapes 5 ro; berries of bryony 5 ro; carob 1/32; honey 1/32; water 1/16; to be strained and drunk for four days. (B 25)

A beverage including bryony and a number of other ingredients was thought to ease pain in the mouth (E 122), and another concoction was used to treat the liver (E 477). Bryony was an ingredient in unguents to treat headache and in various poultices, and along with an unidentified plant it was used to cure a demonic disease by fumigation (Bln 73).

Cannabis sativa L.   Hemp

Ancient Egyptian ⬭𓄿⬭𓄿𓏛 *šmšmt*

Coptic ⲉⲣⲃⲓⲥⲓ

Greek ?

Modern Egyptian Arabic قِنَّب *qinnib*

Hemp is a tall, annual shrub with thin leaves. It grows wild and is cultivated in the Soviet Union and Central Europe for the oily seeds and fibre, and in tropical countries for the flowering tops, which produce marijuana, a narcotic drug.

The plant was known in Egypt by the middle of the second millennium BC, when the fibres were used for ropes, but the word occurs as early as in the Pyramid Texts, written down a thousand years earlier, also in connection with rope making. Pieces of hemp have recently been found in the tomb of Amenophis IV (Akhenaten) at el-Amarna; cannabis pollen has been identified on the mummy of Ramesses II. The medicinal use of hemp is known from a number of prescriptions:

A treatment for the eyes: celery; hemp; is ground and left in the dew overnight. Both eyes of the patient are to be washed with it early in the morning. (Ram III A 26)

It is worth mentioning that in modern herbal medicine hemp is used to treat glaucoma.

A remedy to treat inflammation: leaves [or buds?] of hemp; white oil. Use as an ointment. (Bln 81)

A remedy to cool the uterus: hemp is pounded in honey and administered to the vagina. This is a contraction [of the uterus]. (E 821)

Hemp is employed as an enema with carob (B 24), and with other ingredients in a poultice for a toe nail (E 618).

There is nothing to suggest that the ancient Egyptians had discovered the effect of cannabis when taken or smoked. This on the other hand had been experienced by the Assyrians who in their herbal medicine used it in fumigation to dispel sorrow or grief (§ 10 AT).

Capparis spinosa L.   Caper bush

Ancient Egyptian ?

Coptic ⲔⲈⲠⲈⲖⲈⲞⲤ or ⲔⲈⲠⲀⲢⲒⲤ

Greek κάππαρις

Modern Egyptian Arabic لصّاف *laṣṣâf*; كبار *kabâr*

The caper bush is a shrub with tough round leaves and white or pink single flowers with four petals and numerous stamens. It grows in the Mediterranean and North Africa. The unopened flower buds are known as capers. In a pickled state they are widely used for culinary purposes.

The plant was known to Dioscorides, Theophrastus and Pliny, the latter stating explicitly that it grew in Egypt (*NH*.XIII.xliv). In The Assyrian Herbal a plant called *baltu* has been identified as caper, and finds in Iraq suggest that it existed in that part of the world. The Biblical *avionah* is believed to be the caper bush.

On Egyptian soil it was used medicinally by the Copts to treat a wound, and it is probably merely a question of time until the plant is identified in the ancient Egyptian texts. Powdered root bark is quoted by Prospero Alpini as a treatment for skin ailments, and as a vermifuge and emmenagogue (*Plantes*, 129).

Carthamus tinctorius L.   Safflower

Ancient Egyptian 𓂝𓃀𓆓𓏏𓏤 *k3t3*

Coptic ⲬⲞⲨⲬ

Greek κνῆκος (ἡ ἥμερος)

Modern Egyptian Arabic قرطم *qurṭum*

Safflower is an annual herb with yellow flowers, apparently indigenous to Persia and north-west India, but introduced into Egypt during the New Kingdom if not before. It is frequently mentioned in Ptolemaic texts, and it grows in abundance in the fields today.

The seeds produce a bland oil used for cooking and salads. The flowers yield a yellow colour, soluble in water, and a more permanent red, which has been used for dyeing silk, and in the manufacture of rouge. In some cases present day *kohl* has been shown to consist of the ashes of the safflower plant. The seeds are used as a masticatory.

The ancient Egyptian name for the plant has been identified as *k3t3*, but Dioscorides says that the Egyptians called it *khino* (III. 107). Judging from the occurrence of the Coptic equivalent in the medical texts, one might have expected to find some mention of the herb in pharaonic medical texts, but this is not so. The Copts prescribed it for bandages and as a remedy to be taken:

An old wound if you want it to heal: old, dry safflower; cadmiun; grind it together. Sprinkle it on [the wound], fasten a bandage to it and tie it. It will heal. (Ch 129)

For someone who expels blood: barley flour; flour of safflower; 'scorpion grapes'; boil it to a porridge. The patient shall eat as much as he can. (Ch 228)

Pliny says that the Egyptians did not consume safflower oil, but used it as a protection against poisonous stings: 'the cnecos . . . an Egyptian plant . . . [must be mentioned] for the great help it affords against venomous creatures as well as against venomous fungi. It is a well known fact that as long as they hold this plant, those stung by scorpions feel no sharp pain' (*NH*.XXI. cvii).

Apart from using the seeds for oil and the flowers for dyeing, the Egyptians found the flower pleasing to the eye and included it in the garlands laid on the mummies of their relatives. Remains of safflower were found in the tomb of Tutankhamun.

Safflower seeds. From Kôm Aushîm; Roman. Agricultural Museum, Cairo.

Centaurea depressa M.B.   Cornflower

Ancient Egyptian?

Coptic?

Greek?

Modern Egyptian Arabic (*C. cyanus*) عنبر *'anbar*

Cornflower grows wild in the cornfields of Europe. It is an annual herb with grey leaves and bright-blue flowers. A decoction of the flowers has a mildly astringent effect and is an excellent eye tonic. It has been prescribed for menstrual disorders. The juice of the flower was previously used to make blue ink.

As long as the Egyptian name for the flower has not been identified, its medicinal use in ancient times remains obscure. The flowers were often included in mummy garlands, and it is frequently represented as growing in the gardens as well as in decorative patterns. It is hard to imagine that the Egyptians found no use for it other than decorative.

Cornflower. Wall-painting from Theban Tomb no. 217; Ramesside.

Ceratonia siliqua L.   Carob tree

Ancient Egyptian: tree 𓆸𓏤 *nḏm* ('sweet'); pod pulp? 𓂧𓄿𓂋𓏏𓏥 *ḏ3rt*

Coptic: pod ⲭⲓⲉⲓⲣⲉ or ϭⲁⲡⲁⲧⲉ

Greek: pod κεράτιον; tree κερωνία or συκῆ ἡ Αἰγυπτία ('Egyptian fig')

Modern Egyptian Arabic: tree and pod حروب *ḥarrûb*

The carob tree grows on poor soil in warm climates. The pods are nourishing and contain protein, starch and sugar. They are now used as fodder and in commercially produced beverages. The ground pod is not unlike cocoa in taste and texture and is recommended as a healthier alternative. The gum contained in the seeds (carob gum) is used as a demulcent and lubricant.

Carob trees grew in ancient Egypt. The pods were used to produce sweet carob beer, and in medicine they were part of a vermifuge:

Seeds of carob 1; milk 1; honey 1; rhizomes of cyperus grass ['tiger nuts'] 1; wine; is boiled, strained and drunk for four days. This is to empty the bowels. (E 80)

A remedy to treat worm: carob pod pulp(?) 1/8; red ochre 1/64; fermented plant juice 2½ ro; white oil 1/8; sweet beer 25 ro; is boiled and taken. (E 84)

Carob also found use in the treatment of digestive disorder:

A remedy to stop diarrhoea(?): fresh carob pod pulp(?) 1/8; fresh porridge 1/8; oil or fat; honey 1/4; wax 1/16; water 25 ro; is boiled and eaten for four days. (E 44)

A remedy to treat the anus: carob pod juice(?) 1; honey 1/8; wax 1/16; goose fat 1/8; water 25 ro; is left in the dew overnight and drunk for four days. (E 153)

The meaning of the Egyptian word *ḏ3rt* is somewhat disputed, having been translated either as 'carob pod pulp' or 'colocynth'. The most recent study of the problem suggests that 'carob' is the more likely of the two. Carob pod(?) occurs in countless prescriptions for a surprising number of eye diseases and coughs:

A remedy for curing red inflammation in both eyes: carob pod pulp(?); acacia leaves; green eye paint; milk from a woman who has given birth to a boy; is made into a paste and applied to the lids of both eyes. (E 408)

Another remedy to open the sight by applying something to the lids of the eyes: carob pod pulp(?) 1; the inside of a mussel 1; is mixed with oil or fat, made into a dough and applied to the eye-lids. (E 343)

Another remedy to open the sight: black eye paint; juice of fresh carob pods(?); fermented honey; is applied to both eyes. (E 399)

Another remedy for the eyes: carob pod pulp(?) is ground in fermented honey and applied to the eyes. (Ram III A 24)

A carob tree or an acacia.
Wall-painting in Theban Tomb no.
69; 18th Dynasty.

A remedy to treat a tooth which is eaten away where the gums begin: cumin 1; frankincense 1; carob pod pulp(?) 1; is ground to a powder and applied to the tooth. (E 742)

A remedy to make a wound heal: ibex fat 1; wax 1; carob pod pulp(?) 1; is mixed and used as a bandage. (E 525)

A remedy to dry up a wound: frankincense 1; carob pod pulp(?) 1; ox fat 1; is ground together and applied. (E 520)

A remedy to treat any effluency: boiled barley 1; carob pod pulp(?) 1; frankincense 1; oil or fat 1; is made to a paste and used as a bandage. (E 532)

A remedy to treat the white spots of a burn: powdered carob pod pulp(?); is mixed with honey and used as a bandage. (E 506)

A remedy to treat shaking in any limb of a man: emmer grains 1; carob pod pulp(?) 1; malachite 1; is boiled and applied. (E 626)

A remedy to stop smells in a man or a woman: crushed carob pod pulp(?) is shaped to pellets and the body is anointed with it. (E 709)

The Copts used 'carob water' in medical treatment, but the nature of the disease is not indicated (MK 12). Prospero Alpini informs us that in his day carob was much used to relieve the stomach (*Médicine*, 312). Dioscorides quotes fresh carob pods for this purpose, while the dried pods had the opposite effect (I.158).

Cicer arietinum L.   Chick-pea

Ancient Egyptian 𓄛𓏤𓄿𓏥 *ḥrw bỉk* ('falcon's head')

Coptic ⲉⲣϣⲓϣ or ⲃⲓⲗ ⲛⲉⲃⲱⲕ ('falcon's eye')

Greek ἐρέβινθος

Modern Egyptian Arabic حمص *ḥummuṣ*

Chick-peas are a favourite dish in Egypt today, especially soaked, crushed and mixed with sesame paste and spices. In India they are ground to make *gram* flour for bread and batters. They were also part of the ancient diet. Tutankhamun was given a basket of chick-peas to sustain him in the Hereafter. They are mentioned in texts, but not in a medical context.

The Copts, however, like Dioscorides (II.126) believed them to be stimulating for milk production:

For the breasts so that they give milk: Take 'falcon's eye' and cook it. The patients are to drink the liquid first, then eat the rest. (BA 7)

Ancient Egyptian 𓂝𓏤𓆷 *ḥrỉ*(?)

Coptic 2ρι; wild chicory 2ρι ΝΤΟΟΥ

Greek κιχόριον

Modern Egyptian Arabic هندبا *hendiba*; *C. pumilum* شكورية *šikoria*

Chicory is a deep-rooted perennial growing to 1.5m. The hairy stem has virtually leafless rigid branches; the lower leaves are oblong, partly clasping and bristly beneath. It has large blue flowers which close at noon. It grows wild in Europe, but varieties are cultivated commercially, the lower leaves as a salad herb (endive), and the root for coffee substitute. Among other things it contains inulin, vitamins B, C, K and P. The leaf and root are diuretic and laxative. Chicory has been used to treat jaundice, and the leaves produce a blue dye. Prospero Alpini quotes chicory used as a coffee substitute (*Médicine*, 264). It was considered a 'cooling' herb, the 'endive' mentioned by him to treat feverish diseases, used both internally and externally (*Médicine*, 13, 316–18, 324).

Pliny is our best source for the use of chicory in antiquity. He mentions a 'wild chicory' grown in Egypt along with a cultivated kind (*NH*.XIX.xxxix; XX. xxix; cf. also XXI.lii). The juice, he says, used with rose oil and vinegar relieves headache; it was drunk with wine to treat the liver and bladder, a use reflected in more recent herbal medicine.

Dioscorides quotes the Egyptian name for chicory as *agon* (II.160); according to Pliny the wild kind was called *seris*. The word *ḥrỉ* does not occur in any of the medical texts, but it is virtually identical to the Coptic designation for chicory. The Copts used a mixture of ground chicory, linseed, salt and tragacanth as a poultice for swollen glands (Ch 223), and it was included in a remedy to treat blood spitting (see above, under Acacia).

Ancient Egyptian 𓍿𓈖𓆷𓊪𓋴 *tỉ-šps*

Coptic ΚΙΝΑΜШΜΟΝ

Greek κινάμωμον

Modern Egyptian Arabic قرفة *qirfa*

The latest research (1988) suggests the East African camphor tree (*Cinnamonium camphora* or *Ocotea usambarensis*) for *tỉ-šps*. The constituents of the roots of *C. zeylanicum* and *C. camphora* are very similar, but traditionally *tỉ-šps* is taken to mean cinnamon. In the classical texts cinnamon is often confused with cassia

(*Cinnamonium cassia*). The Egyptian texts may not make the distinction either. The two are very similar to each other. The *C. zeylanicum* tree is smaller than cassia, and the quills of bark are thinner and more fragile. The flavour of cassia is more pungent. Even in a powdered state, the two can be distinguished under a microscope. Prospero Alpini knew thin quills as *qirfa*, whereas thick quills were called *dârsîni*.

The evergreen cinnamon tree is native to Ceylon, whereas cassia originated in China and Burma. It was thus imported into Egypt. Cinnamon is stimulant, digestive and antiseptic. A tea made of cinnamon, water and sugar is widely drunk in the Middle East in cold weather. Another winter drink is made from milk, powdered resin, chopped pistachios and cinnamon. In Europe it is a favourite addition to puddings and cakes, in Mediterranean countries also for dishes including tomatoes, and it is an ingredient in curry spice. The 'buds' (immature fruits) of cassia are used for scenting potpourri and for commercially produced sweets and beverages.

Both cinnamon and cassia are mentioned in the Bible. The classical sources mention cinnamon as an ingredient in Egyptian perfume. Theophrastus, for instance, says that a perfume called *megaleion* was made of burnt resin and balanos oil to which is added cassia, cinnamon and myrrh: 'This perfume and the Egyptian are the most troublesome to make, since no others involve the mixture of so many and such costly ingredients. To make *megaleion*, they say, the oil is boiled for ten days and nights, and not till then do they put in the resin and the other things, since the oil is more receptive when it has been thoroughly boiled' (*Concerning Odours* VI.30).

There is no record from pharaonic Egypt of cinnamon having been taken internally for any purpose. But there are prescriptions for cinnamon unguents, where the characteristic scent and the antiseptic qualities would be appreciated:

An unguent to soothe the members: *kohl* 1; wax 1; frankincense 1; cinnamon 1; dry myrrh 1; ox fat 1; sweet moringa oil 1; to be used as a poultice for four days. (E 687)

A remedy to make flesh grow: carob pod pulp(?) 1; beans 1; cinnamon 1; oil or fat 1; honey 1; is ground together and [the member] is bandaged therewith. (E 534)

A remedy to heal every affluency: goat's fat 1; wax 1; fragrant gum 1; cinnamon 1; fresh moringa oil 1; is mixed and applied to the effluency until it is healed. (E 540)

A remedy for destruction of an eating ulcer on the gums: cinnamon 1; gum 1; honey 1; oil or fat 1; to be used as a bandage. (E 553)

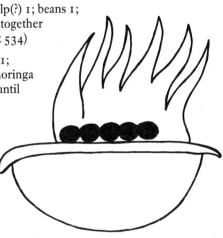

Burning incense; cinnamon was used in incense. Wall-painting in the tomb of Queen Nefertari, Thebes; Ramesside.

Cinnamon was one of the ingredients in a suppository 'to cool the anus', made up from equal parts of juniper berries, frankincense, ochre, cumin, cinnamon, honey, myrrh and three unidentified ingredients (E 140).

As we have seen, the wood of cinnamon was used in a fumigation 'which one makes to make the smell of the house or the dress pleasant'. It may be added that cinnamon is an ingredient in one of the modern brands of natural toothpaste.

Cinnamon or cassia are the only true spices actually to be mentioned in connection with mummification. Diodorus described how after cleaning the body with palm wine and (unspecified) spices and anointing it with 'cedar oil' (probably oil of juniper) and other unguents it was then rubbed with myrrh, cinnamon and other materials to preserve it. What appears to be cinnamon has been found on actual mummies, although the statements cannot at present be verified. A mummy from the 20th Dynasty is described as having 'a thick layer of spicery covering every part of it . . . this external covering, which is nowhere less than an inch in thickness and which is interposed everywhere between the bandages and the skin . . . still retains the faint smell of cinnamon or cassia . . . but when mixed with alcohol or water and exposed to the action of heat the odour of myrrh becomes very powerfully predominant.' (Osburn, quoted in Lucas, *Anc. Eg. Mat.*, pp. 308–9). Another mummy examined in the last century was also said to be filled with the 'dust of cedar, cassia, etc.' (Pettigrew, quoted *ibid.*, p. 309).

Cinnamon was among the items presented to the temples by the king. In a papyrus listing the revenue ceded to the various gods by Ramesses III, there is frequent mention of measures of cinnamon. Once in the temple, the goods would pass into the hands of the priests who would either recirculate them in exchange for other commodities, or, since they formed the medical profession as

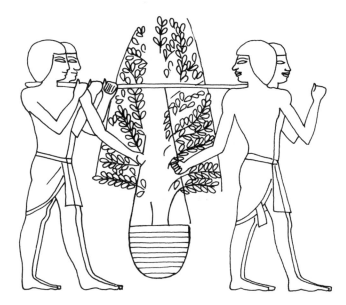

Loading incense trees: Queen Hatshepsut's expedition to Punt returned with spices and fragrant woods. Relief in the temple of Hatshepsut at Deir el-Bahari; 18th Dynasty.

well, use it in their preparations of drugs. There is no evidence of it having been burnt in front of the god whose property it was. The king's gift to the god Amun included one whole log, 246 measures and 82 bundles. When new feasts were instituted by the king 220 bundles and 155 measures were included among the allowances.

Earlier on, in the 18th Dynasty, when Queen Hatshepsut sent out her famous expedition to the land of Punt in search of incense and spices, the ships were loaded for their homeward journey not only with frankincense and myrrh, but with other fragrant woods, including cinnamon. Wherever the land of Punt may have been located, cinnamon trees did not grow there. Punt was once part of the chain of commerce which spread from the East to Africa and Europe, and cinnamon was one of the costly commodities which made the long journey. In the 19th Dynasty Sethos I also connects cinnamon with Punt when displaying to the god Amun how he has conquered the world: 'I turn my face to the East, I work a wonder for you . . . I gather together all the countries of Punt, all their tribute of gum and myrrh and cinnamon and all the pleasant sweet wood of the God's land'.

Citrullus colocynthus (L.) Schrad.   Colocynth

Ancient Egyptian ?

Coptic ⲗⲁⲕⲁⲙⲟⲩ or ⲭⲱⲛⲭ

Greek ?

Modern Egyptian Arabic حنظل *ḥanzal*

Colocynth appears to be native to Egypt, where it still grows in the desert. It is a perennial creeping herb with long trailing branches. The fleshy fruits, the size of an orange or smaller, are uniform or mottled with dark green, turning yellow when ripe. They are extremely bitter. The dried and powdered pulp is a powerful hydragogue cathartic, and is toxic in large doses. An oil used to be extracted from the seeds, but it is no longer in use.

The Egyptian word *ḏ3rt*, occurring frequently in the medical texts, has frequently been identified with colocynth, but it seems that 'carob' is more appropriate. This means, however, that until another word has been offered for 'colocynth' we do not know to what extent it was used in ancient Egyptian medicine. In Akkadian it was known as *tigillu* and in Hebrew possibly as *paqqūʿot*.

Citrullus lanatus (Thunb.) Mansf.
Citrullus colocynthoïdes Schw.

Water melon

Ancient Egyptian ⟨hieroglyphs⟩ *bddw-k3*(?)

Coptic ?

Greek μελοπέπον

Modern Egyptian Arabic: fruit of *C. lanatus* بطيخ *battyḥ*; seeds لب *libb*; fruit of *C. colocynthoïdes* جورمة *gurma*

Water melons grow in dry, tropical climates. *C. colocynthoïdes* was cultivated from early times in Egypt, possibly from the Old Kingdom. *C. lanatus* may not have been developed until much later. The fruit and the roasted seeds are widely consumed in the Middle East, and an oil can be extracted from the seeds.

The ancient name for the plant was probably *bddw-k3*. It occurs in a number of prescriptions:

A remedy to treat trembling fingers: rub the finger with oil or fat and bandage it with *bddw-k3*. (H 205)

A remedy for constipation: zizyphus bread 1; *bddw-k3* 1; cat's dung 1; sweet beer 1; wine 1; combine to a paste and use as a bandage. (E 208)

A remedy to expel a disease caused by a demon: *bddw-k3*; wine; drink it. (Bln 111)

To recognise a woman who will give birth as opposed to a woman who will not give birth: *bddw-k3* is ground and mixed with milk from a woman who has given birth to a boy. Make it into a drink for the woman and let her drink it. If she vomits she will give birth. If she swells up, she will never give birth. (Bln 193)

What is further said about it as a treatment: *bddw-k3* is mixed with milk from a woman who has given birth to a boy. Inject it into her vulva. If she vomits, she will give birth. If she swells up, it means that she will not give birth. (Bln 194)

Bddw-k3 occurs in a mythological context also connected with fertility. On one occasion when the god Seth is pursuing the beautiful Isis and has transformed himself into a bull, he scatters his semen on the ground in frustration. From it grew the plants called *bddw-k3*. The way in which the word is written in hieroglyphs (see above) may account for the particular properties attributed to the plant.

Prospero Alpini mentions water melon in connection with remedies used by Egyptian women to gain weight.

A water melon.
Wall-painting in a tomb at
Meir; Old Kingdom.

Myrobalanos (dried fruit from India) is macerated in water melon pulp for one night. The women were told to take an ounce of this a day every morning before breakfast (*Médicine*, 235).

Convulvulus scammonia L.   Convolvulus

Ancient Egyptian 𓏏𓄿𓂋𓈖𓏏𓏏 *snwtt* (?)
Coptic ⲥⲕⲁⲙⲟⲩⲛⲓⲁ
Greek σκαμμονία
Modern Egyptian Arabic ?

This convolvulus is a twining shrub growing to 4 or 5m, with large ochre-yellow funnel-shaped flowers and cordeate leaves, sometimes incised-lobed. The plant is described by Theophrastus who says that the gum of the plant occurs in its root (IX.1.3), and that its juice has (unspecified) medicinal properties (IX.1.4). The Copts used it as a purgative (Ch 74 and 76) and as an ingredient in an ointment (ZB 29). Dioscorides refers to the Egyptian names of three plants which have been identified as *C. scammonia (oxioui)*, *C. farinosus (saneloum)*, and *C. arvensis (toukou)* (IV.171; IV.14), but this has brought us no closer to establishing its use in ancient Egypt.

Cordia myxa L.   Egyptian plum

Ancient Egyptian ?
Coptic ?
Greek κοκκυμηλέα (ἡ Αἰγυπτία)
Modern Egyptian Arabic مخيط *muḫêṭ*

The tree grows to about 5m, carrying orange fruits. It is found wild in India and is cultivated in Egyptian gardens. The fruit ('sebesten') is used in folk medicine as a laxative and as a soothing remedy for pulmonary ailments.

Theophrastus gave a detailed description of the tree and says that the people of Upper Egypt harvest so many plums that they dry them, remove the stones, bruise the pulp and make cakes of it (IV.2.10). Pliny adds that the fruit was used for making wine (*NH*.XIII.10).

The ancient Egyptian name has not yet been identified. As well as being eaten, the fruit was probably used in pharaonic medicine. In the days of Prospero Alpini the mashed and reduced pulp was considered emollient and was used to treat coughs and tumours, among other things (*Plantes*, 29).

Ancient Egyptian ⌗𓇥𓏛𓏥 *š3w*
Coptic ⲃⲉⲣϣϩⲟⲩ
Greek κορίαννον
Modern Egyptian Arabic كسبرة *kusbara*

This umbelliferous herb is cultivated throughout the world. Apart from the use of the fresh leaves and dried seeds in cooking, coriander has a variety of uses in modern herbal medicine. It is a stimulant, carminative and digestive and is used for coughs and in bandages for rheumatism. In medieval times it was an ingredient in love potions. Prospero Alpini commented on its 'cooling' effect: it was added to a lukewarm bath to expel fever. The seeds were used with other herbs in a potion to treat fever and flatulence (*Médicine*, 246, 313). Furthermore, no dish was cooked without the addition of coriander leaves (*Plantes*, 131).

Pliny praises the quality of Egyptian coriander: 'The best, as is generally agreed, is the Egyptian. It is an antidote for the poison of the two-headed serpent, the amphisbaena, both taken in drink and applied . . . Spreading sores also are healed by coriander with honey or raisins, likewise diseased testes, burns, carbuncles, and sore ears, fluxes of the eyes, too, if woman's milk be added. It is also taken in drink with rue for cholera. Intestinal parasites are expelled by coriander seed' (*NH*.xx.lxxxii). Apicius mentions coriander along with cumin to flavour fish and marrows (III.4.3; x.1.7–8).

A number of extant prescriptions prove the statement by Pliny on the medicinal use of the herb among the Egyptians. The inevitable stomach ailments could be cured by a beverage mixed from coriander, flax, dates, grass, bryony and beer (see prescription under *Bryonia*). If a man had blood coming out (presumably in the stools), the mixture was to include coriander, chaste-tree and an unidentified fruit, all grated, mixed with honey and beer and strained (Bln 188). An obscure illness which was believed to be a kind of spell cast by a god or by a dead man was eased by a mixture of figs, celery, honey, grapes, zizyphus bread, and three unidentified plant ingredients, to be taken before going to sleep (E 226 = H 84). If a broken bone needed bandaging, the prescription included coriander, honey, fermented plant juice and an unidentified plant, pounded to a paste and applied (H 220). Coriander was included in unguents, among others one to treat herpes:

A remedy for it: fermented honey; dry myrrh; coriander seeds; is ground in dregs and used for anointing. (H 161)

Coriander was among the herbs offered to the temple by the king. Some seeds were found in the tomb of Tutankhamun, and others have been discovered elsewhere.

Ancient Egyptian 𓇑𓈙𓏏 *šspt*

Coptic ϣⲱⲡⲉ or ⲗⲟⲙⲱⲡⲉⲣⲟⲛ (from Greek μελοπέπον)

Greek ?

Modern Egyptian Arabic عجور *ʿaggûr*

The Greeks, the Romans and the Assyrians had no special word for melon, which they simply called 'ripe (cucumber)', and there has in the past been some confusion between the two which to a modern consumer are quite different. The ancient Egyptians, however, appear to have made the distinction (for 'cucumber' see the following entry). Apart from being part of the Egyptian diet, melon found use in medicine:

A remedy to treat the heart: *šspt*-melon 1/32; notched sycamore fruits 5 ro; ochre 1/32; fresh dates 5 ro; honey 5 ro; water 20 ro; is left in the dew overnight, strained and drunk for one day. (E 220)

Melon leaves were part of mixtures to be taken for bladder ailments and other diseases of the stomach or anus. The fruit was used in a prescription for depilation (cf. above, under 'Cosmetics'). The Copts used the fruit in soothing applications:

If you take a ϣⲱⲡⲉ-melon, boil it and anoint inflamed legs with it, they will heal. (ZB 7)

If you take a roasted ϣⲱⲡⲉ-melon and grind it with aloe and add wine and anoint the afflicted spot with it, it will heal. (ZB 10)

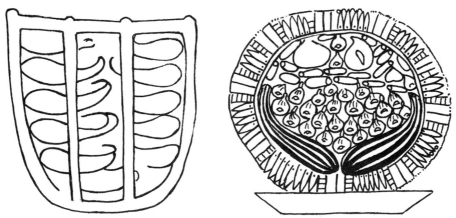

(*Above left*) A basket of cucumbers or melons. Wall-painting in Theban Tomb no. 52; 18th Dynasty.

(*Above right*) A basket(?) containing melons, figs and dates. Wall-painting in Theban Tomb no. 217; Ramesside.

Ancient Egyptian ⌐𝄞⌐ *bndt* (?)

Coptic ⲃⲟⲛⲧⲉ

Greek ?

Modern Egyptian Arabic خيار *ḥiâr,* عبد الاوي *'abd el-lawy;*
small cucumber خيار قسة *ḥiâr qassa*

Cucumbers are abundantly represented on Egyptian monuments, and seeds
have been found in excavations, probably of the small *Chate* variety which still
grows in the Sudan. If *šspt* is melon (see above), we are left without a word for
cucumber in the medical texts. In view of the popularity of the plant, and
considering the widespread use of its astringent properties in modern herbal
applications, this is peculiar. The Copts used ⲃⲟⲛⲧⲉ in medicine:

Take leaves of ⲃⲟⲛⲧⲉ, sprinkle(?) with salt and place on the breasts. They will become
full of milk. (BA 10)

The word ⲃⲟⲛⲧⲉ would appear to be a descendant of ancient Egyptian
bndt, for which, however, no medical use has been recorded. In traditional
Islamic medicine cucumber leaves soothed the bite of a mad dog; the dried and
pounded seeds found use as a dentifrice; and if steeped in water and squeezed
they were used in treatment of the bladder.

A cucumber(?).
Wall-painting in
Theban Tomb no. 52;
18th Dynasty.

Cumin cyminum L.   Cumin

Ancient Egyptian 𐦀𐦀 *tpnn*

Coptic ⲧⲁⲡⲛ

Greek κύμινον

Modern Egyptian Arabic كمون *kammûn*

This annual umbelliferous herb is indigenous to Egypt. The seeds are stimulant
and carminative and are widely used for flavouring (particularly curries) and in
the perfume industry. In Egypt today it is one of the favourite spices for a great

number of traditional dishes. Women who have recently given birth add it to a beverage, and it is used for indigestion and colic.

Pliny described the excellent quality of Egyptian cumin: 'Of all the seasonings which gratify a fastidious taste cumin is the most agreeable . . . Another kind of cumin is the wild variety called country cumin or by other people Thebaic cumin. For pounding up in water and using it as a draught in case of stomach ache the most highly esteemed kind in our continent is that grown in Carpetania, though elsewhere the prize is awarded to Ethiopian and African cumin; however some prefer the Egyptian to the African.' (*NH*.XIX.xlvii)

The Egyptians in the days of Apicius used to flavour marrows and fish with cumin (III.4.3; X.1.6), along with coriander, a combination of which is reminiscent of curry mixtures. Pliny says that cumin was strewn under (!) bread and used to flavour an Alexandrian sauce (*NH*.XIX.xlvii). Cumin was among the offerings presented by Ramesses III to the temple of Re at Heliopolis. Contemporary seeds have been found in the village of Deir el-Medîna.

The medicinal properties of cumin were widely recognised in Egyptian medicine. In modern herbal medicine cumin is used to treat digestive problems, an efficient remedy as both Pliny and the Egyptians had noticed:

A remedy for the belly when it is ill: cumin 1/64; goose fat 1/8; milk 20 ro; is boiled, strained and taken. (E 5 = H 55)

A remedy to calm a cough: set milk; cumin; is mixed with honey and eaten by the patient for four days. (Bln 31)

A remedy to treat the chest: carob pod pulp(?) 1/16; cumin 1/4; wine; is boiled and drunk for four days. (E 183)

To treat a tongue which is ill: frankincense 1; cumin 1; yellow ochre 1; goose fat 1; honey 1; water 1; to be chewed and spat out. (E 700)

A remedy to kill pain in all parts of the body: frankincense 1/64; cumin 1/64; fresh bread 1/8; goose fat 1/16; honey 1/16; sweet beer 20 ro; is strained and drunk for four days. (H 43)

A remedy to dry out the ear when water comes out of it: red ochre 1; cumin 1; 'donkey's ear' [plant] 1; best unguent 1; moringa oil 1; is dripped into the ear. (E 770)

To be applied as a poultice after an enema: myrrh 1; goose fat 1; cumin 1; frankincense 1; honey 1; combine and apply so that the patient gets well. (B 12,6,1–2)

A remedy to remove heat in the anus: antelope fat 1; cumin 1; to be made into a suppository and inserted. (E 142)

A remedy to treat a tooth which is being eaten away at the gum: cumin 1; frankincense 1; carob pod pulp(?) 1; make it into a powder and apply to the tooth. (E 742)

Cumin was furthermore included in a prescription for an unguent to ease headache, which was made of moringa oil, myrrh, lotus flowers, juniper berries and two unidentified ingredients (E 258).

The Copts used a mixture of roasted cumin and parsley ground with egg to treat a swollen belly (Ch 71). For flatulence, cumin, pepper, rue, senna, natron and honey were ground together and taken (Ch 69). The fumes of boiled cumin were thought to heal a 'fixed' uterus when the patient was made to squat over it (Ch 125).

The Assyrian Herbal recommends the use of cumin in anointing, eye poultices and for insect stings (§ 10 M).

Cyperus esculentus L.   Cyperus grass

Ancient Egyptian: plant ꜣ𓏤𓏛 *giw*; rhizome 𓃀𓏛 *wꜥḥ* or 𓂝𓏛 *šnỉ-t3*

Coptic ВІКХІ

Greek μαλιναθάλλη

Modern Egyptian Arabic: plant سعد *suꜥd*; rhizome حب العزيز *ḥabb el-aziz*

Cyperus grass is distinguished by its pale spikelets and fibrous root system and ovoid tubers. It grows in moist soils or on sandy sea-shores. In Egypt it is now cultivated for its edible tubers ('tiger nuts') which are first dried, then soaked in water. The taste is not unlike that of hazelnuts. In certain parts of Spain a drink made from the tubers is extremely popular. Called *horchata di chufa* it is reminiscent of a milk shake.

Theophrastus said that the plant was called *mnasion* by the Egyptians and that it was sweet and only used for food (IV.8.2). The tubers were consumed by the earliest inhabitants of the Nile Valley, and remains of them have been found in the stomach contents of prehistoric bodies. In the New Kingdom they are known to have been ground and mixed with honey to make a delicious sweetmeat (see above, under 'In the kitchen').

Measuring tiger nuts. Wall-painting in Theban Tomb no. 100; 18th Dynasty.

Cyperus papyrus L.   Papyrus

Ancient Egyptian 𓈖𓏏𓏥 *mhyt* or 𓆱𓏏𓏥 *twfy*

Coptic: plant ⲭⲟⲟⲩϥ; paper ⲭⲁⲣⲧⲏⲥ

Greek: plant πάπυρος; also βύβλος; paper χάρτης

Modern Egyptian Arabic بردي *burdi*

Now only cultivated in Egyptian gardens (although it has recently been discovered growing spontaneously in the Wâdi Natrûn), papyrus grew in abundance along the River Nile in ancient times. The plant had multiple uses. The
pith was peeled and arranged in sheets, two being beaten together to make
writing material. The fibres were woven into sail and cloth and mats, or twisted
into ropes, or plaited into sandals. Jar-stoppers and children's balls of papyrus
have been found. The mature stems were tied together and made into boats, or
they were used as fire wood. The feathery flowers on their long stems were the
ideal base for tall composite bouquets used to decorate temples and tombs, and
the stalks were edible. Herodotus tells that the lower extremity of the plant,
about one cubit of it (about half a metre), was a delicacy particularly when first
baked in a glowing hot vessel on the fire (II.92). Theophrastus adds that all the

(*Right*) A bouquet of papyrus, lotus, mandrake
and poppy before the mummy. Wall-painting in
Theban Tomb no. 181; 18th Dynasty.

(*Above*) Papyrus. Wall-painting in the royal palace at el-Amarna; 18th Dynasty.

natives 'chew the papyrus raw, boiled or roasted; they swallow the juice and spit out the quid' (IV.8.4), exactly like the Egyptians do with sugar cane today. Diodorus mentions children being given the stalks, roasted in the coals, and the roots or stems of (other) marsh plants either raw, boiled or baked (I.80.5). Dioscorides also comments on papyrus chewing (I.115).

In pharaonic medicine papyrus was used with other herbs in a bandage for stiff limbs (E 669) and in an eye compress (E 340). It is interesting to note Pliny's observation that dried papyrus was used for expanding and drying fistulae and opening them to other remedies, and that the plant itself, applied with water, cured callosities (NH.XXIX.li.lxxxviii). Similar uses were quoted by Prospero Alpini (Plantes, 110).

The Copts used the ashes of the plant, i.e. burnt sheets of papyrus. A toothpowder was made of: orpiment, metal chips, sulphur, burnt papyrus, lead, and salt (Ch 178). A tumour was treated with a powder consisting of burnt papyrus, incense and another plant (Ch 121). Pliny indicates that this way of using papyrus was older than the Copts: the paper made from it (i.e. the plant) was when burnt one of the caustic remedies: its ash was taken in wine to induce sleep (NH.XXIV.li). It is worth mentioning that in traditional Islamic medicine the ashes of papyrus matting were applied to open wounds to dry them out, the ashes being also considered beneficial for sores of the mouth, and, mixed with vinegar, to treat nose-bleed.

Elettaria cardamomum (L.) Maton   Cardamom

Ancient Egyptian ?

Coptic ?

Greek καρδάμωμον

Modern Egyptian Arabic حبهان‎ *ḥabahân*

The cardamom tree is indigenous to India and Ceylon. No ancient Egyptian name for it has been identified, nor have traces of it been found, but classical sources mention it as an ingredient in the much-valued Egyptian unguents. Pliny informs us that the best one was made in the city of Mendes (cf. above, under 'Perfume'). Theophrastus mentions that cardamom was imported into his country from Media, though some said India (IX.7.2), and that it found use in perfumes.

Cardamom seeds have a rich warm flavour used to spice sweet or savoury dishes. It is an important ingredient in curry spice. In Arab countries a few seeds are sometimes added to a cup of coffee. In Scandinavia the seeds lend their characteristic aroma to bread and mulled wine. When chewed, they help digestion and stimulate the appetite.

Ensete ventricosum (Welw.) Cheesman   Wild banana

Ancient Egyptian ?

Coptic ?

Greek ?

Modern Egyptian Arabic: cultivated banana موز *môz*

These wild bananas grow in moist places in the uplands of Ethiopia and East Africa. The fruits are inedible, but people consume the starchy leaf bases. Unlike the cultivated banana, wild bananas are annuals.

One of the nameless plants mentioned by Theophrastus (IV.4.5) as growing in India has been identified as banana. Some people have identified plants depicted on prehistoric pots as wild banana, but this has not been unanimously accepted, cultivated bananas being otherwise unknown in Egypt until the fifth century AD. But recent examination of the residue in a beer vessel from around 1400 BC seems to suggest that yeast cells grown on wild bananas had been used to produce fermentation of the beer.

Prospero Alpini lists a different variety of banana as one of the ingredients in a purgative enema (*Médicine*, 313), and he refers to its supposed aphrodisiac properties (*Plantes*, 78).

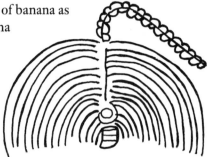

A wild banana(?) painted on a Predynastic pot.

Ferula foetida Regel   Asafoetida

Ancient Egyptian: gum ⌂𓏌𓏤 *gsfn*

Coptic ⲍⲉⲗⲑⲓⲑ

Greek νάρθηξ

Arabic: gum حلتيت *ḥiltit*; root محروت *maḥrût*

The plant is a herbaceous umbelliferous perennial 1.5 to 2m high. It is native to Persia. The strongly foetid brownish gum is collected commercially from plants at least five years old. It is stimulant, anti-spasmodic, expectorant and carminative. It has been prescribed for certain nervous conditions, bronchitis, asthma and flatulence. It is used as a condiment now as it was in ancient Rome, where it was both expensive and highly appreciated. The Assyrian Herbal mentions the herb (called *tiyâtu* or *nuḫustu*) as growing near Babylon (§ 10 CU). The Coptic herbalists prescribed it as an ingredient in a composite eye ointment (Ch 56).

The word *gsfn* has by some been interpreted as an item of mineral origin, whereas others prefer to translate it asafoetida. It occurs in prescriptions for the eye, as for example:

kohl 1; green eye paint 1; carob pod pulp(?) 1; aloe 1; asafoetida gum (?) 1; is mixed with water and applied to the eyes. (E 355)

Ficus carica L.   Fig

Ancient Egyptian ⌂𓇳𓏥: *d3b*; ⌂𓏲𓏲𓏛 *knti*

Coptic ⲕⲛⲧⲉ

Greek συκῆ

Modern Egyptian Arabic تين *tyn*

In Egypt the fig still grows along the Mediterranean. The fruits are eaten fresh, dried or candied. They have a well-known laxative effect. The ancient Egyptians had also observed its properties:

Make a beverage for a patient suffering from constipation: figs 1/8; milk 1/16; notched sycamore figs 1/8; leave it overnight in sweet beer 10 ro. Strain, give it to him to drink very often, and he will soon get well. (E 202)

Another remedy to remove disease in the belly: figs 1/32; Lower Egyptian salt 1/8; fresh bread 1/8; sweet beer 25 ro; is boiled, strained and taken for one day. (E 92)

Picking figs.
Relief in the tomb of
Niankhkhnum and
Khnumhotep at Saqqara;
Old Kingdom.

Figs were used in remedies to treat the heart:

A remedy to treat the heart, truly: figs 1; ochre 1/32; acacia leaves 1/32; honey 1/64; water 25 ro; is strained, left in the dew overnight and drunk for four days. (Bln 117)

Another remedy for the heart: figs 1/8; wheat porridge 1/8; honey 1/8; ochre 1/32; water 25 ro; is boiled and taken for four days. (E 234)

In one instance a lung complaint is treated with a maceration including figs:

Quick acting beverage to treat the lung: ochre 1/32; gum 1/32; honey 1/8; figs 1/8; water 25 ro; is left in the dew overnight and drunk for four days. (H 57)

A heart disease caused by a demon required a soothing drink of:

figs, grapes, notched sycamore figs, honey and cow's milk; is boiled, strained and taken. (Bln 114)

A pain in the anus was treated with a suppository made of:

figs 1; Lower Egyptian salt 1; frankincense 1; ox marrow 1; is made into a suppository and inserted. (E 141)

In Coptic medicine fig leaves, natron, sulphur and honey were rubbed on the skin to treat inflammation (ZB 17), and a patient suffering from haemorrhoids applied 'juice' of fig tree to make them retract (TM) (the latex is a skin irritant, but perhaps the juice of the fruit was meant). Dioscorides gives an indication of how milk was made to set in ancient times. Fig juice made milk coagulate in the manner of rennet (I.183). In a later paragraph he describes how to make a junket by stirring milk over the fire with a freshly cut branch of a fig tree (II.77).

Ficus sycomorus L.   Sycamore fig

Ancient Egyptian: tree 𓏏𓆱 *nht*; notched, ripe fruit 𓈖𓎡𓏏 *nk' wt*; unripe fruit 𓎡𓂝𓏏 *k3w*

Coptic: tree ΝΟΥϨЄ; fruit ЄΛΚШ

Greek συκάμινος Αἰγύπτια

Modern Egyptian Arabic جميز *gimmêz*

Sycamore figs and sycamore wood have been found in predynastic tombs, and the tree is frequently represented in reliefs and wall-paintings of the New Kingdom. To make it edible, the ripe fruit must be 'notched' with a knife before being picked to allow the parasites inside to escape.

The wood was used for timber, and the leaves and particularly the fruit found ample use in pharaonic medicine. The crushed leaves were included in potions to treat constipation (E 210), and in an unguent with ochre, frankincense, myrrh, wax, honey and an unidentified fruit (Bln 95). When a broken bone had been mended, a cooling bandage was applied consisting of:

leaves of acacia; leaves of willow; leaves of sycamore; emmer grains; gum water; bandage for four days. (H 234)

The notched, ripe fruits were a favourite laxative:

To treat a swollen belly: sweet beer remains overnight with notched sycamore fruits. Is eaten and drunk for four days. (E 207b)

Another remedy to empty the belly: cow's milk 1; notched sycamore fruits 1; honey 1; is ground finely, boiled and taken for four days. (E 18)

A remedy to kill worm: dry unripe sycamore fruits 1; fresh dates 1; is finely chopped, placed in thick beer and drunk by the patient. (E 65)

The figs were included as a vehicle for a remedy for toothache:

notched sycamore fruits 1; beans 1; honey 1; malachite 1; ochre 1; is ground to powder and placed on the tooth. (E 741)

Chewing-gum to treat the tongue was made from notched sycamore figs, Lower Egyptian salt, carob pod pulp(?), honey, water and an unidentified ingredient (E 702). Stiff limbs were treated with a bandage of:

clay 1; Lower Egyptian salt 1; sweet beer 1; sycamore fruit 1; is boiled and used as a bandage. (E 676)

Twig of sycamore; Ramesside. Agricultural Museum, Cairo.

If the complaint was a moving 'vessel' the bandage was prescribed to contain:

fruit of sycamore 1; dregs of sweet beer 1; is boiled and applied as a bandage. (E 683)

A painful tumour was treated with fly dung mixed with sycamore juice 'applied to the tumour so that it goes down by itself' (E 570). The 'juice' in question was presumably the sap of the trunk. The method of extracting it was described by Dioscorides (1.181): '. . . the tree is juiced at the first entrance of the spring before it brings forth fruit, the outside of the bark being broken with a stone, for if it is broken further in, it sends nothing forth. The tears of it are gathered in a sponge or fleece, which being dried and formed [into little balls] is stored in a vase.' Its use in medicine was continued by the Copts, who recommended it for rubbing onto any kind of swelling (WM 27). In Egyptian folk medicine at the end of the last century this 'milk of sycamore' was used to treat a number of skin ailments. The effect was presumably due to the fact that the juice sealed off the bacteria in the air.

Bird among sycamore figs. Wall-painting in Theban Tomb no. 51; Ramesside.

Foeniculum vulgare Mill.   Fennel

Ancient Egyptian ?

Coptic ϣⲁⲙⲁⲣ

Greek μάραθον

Modern Egyptian Arabic شمر *šamar* or رازيانيج *râzîânîg*

Fennel is an umbelliferous herb native to the Mediterranean and extensively cultivated for culinary purposes (roots, stalks, leaves and seeds). It is carminative and diuretic.

Although no ancient name for the herb has as yet been identified with any certainty we may assume that it was known and used in ancient times. Several Coptic prescriptions include fennel in the treatment of eye ailments, just as it was recommended in later Egyptian herbals. One of the remedies came as a powder:

A powder for the eyes which suffer from any disease: yellow myrobalanos [dried fruits] 7 drachma; oxide of zinc 7 drachma; grind it together and place it in a jar, [then] in a stone vessel. Leave it for one day and one night. Take it out and grind it. Add acacia gum 1 drachme. Grind it, and for seven days add fennel juice. Use it as a powder. (Ch 90)

There was a quicker prescription for misty eyes:

For one whose eyes are blurred: gall of a black Labes-fish; sycamore honey; fennel juice; mix and apply. (Ch 113)

It is not clear whether pressed fennel juice or an infusion is meant.

Apart from the traditional use in eye medicine, fennel seeds are used as a digestive. In Greece the herb was believed to aid slimming, a use reflected in herbals of much later date. In several ancient civilisations fennel was used as an antidote for snake bite.

Glycyrrhiza glabra L.   Liquorice

Ancient Egyptian ?

Coptic ?

Greek γλυκεία (ῥιζα) ('sweet root')

Modern Egyptian Arabic سوس *sôs*

Liquorice is a herbaceous plant growing to 1.5m, with lilac flowers. The tap-root divides into subsidiary roots 1.25m in length and horizontal stolons which can be up to 8m. It grows wild in Eastern Europe and is now cultivated in many countries. The root is demulcent, expectorant, laxative and antiflammatory. It is used to treat coughs and bronchitis, gastric ulcers and as an eye lotion. It is employed to sweeten medicine, to flavour beer, confectionery and tobacco. In modern Egypt it is made into a traditional beverage sold by street vendors ('erqesôs'). Prospero Alpini quoted liquorice as a 'warming' plant (*Médicine*, 253). Boiled in water with fennel seeds it was used to aid vomiting (*Médicine*, 239).

Pliny says that the boiled-down root was used for pessaries; pounded, it was used as a liniment to treat wounds; and in a powdered state it was chewed by those suffering from mouth ulcers (*NH*.XXII.xi). Theophrastus tells that liquorice, which he calls 'Scythian root', was useful for treating asthma, dry cough and chest troubles; it was thought to be thirst-quenching when used as a masticatory, and with honey it was applied to wounds (IX.13.1), all treatments anticipating the more recent use of the herb. The Assyrian Herbal includes it under the name *šûšu* in treatments for the feet, swellings, excess of saliva and as a diuretic (§ 71).

Considering this wide use it is surprising that no word for liquorice has yet been identified in Coptic or ancient Egyptian medical texts.

Hordeum vulgare L.   Barley

Ancient Egyptian ⸖ *it*

Coptic ⲈⲓⲰⲦ

Greek κριθή

Modern Egyptian Arabic شعير *šíˁyr*

Egyptian barley was chiefly of the four-eared or six-eared variety, although others are occasionally found. It was one of the basic food plants in ancient times, being used for bread and beer. Barley grains have been found dating back to predynastic times. An entire barley plant had been left in the coffin of Amenophis I. Barley sprouts found during excavations were part of the burial rites, being symbolic of the resurrection of Osiris, King of the Dead, but they may well have been consumed by the living as well. Germinated barley was used to produce malt for brewing beer. This was done at home by the housewife or the servants. The resulting fermented liquid was probably like a thin gruel. In present-day Egypt the Nubians brew a kind of beer called *bouza*, which was undoubtedly very similar to that prepared in ancient times. It contains about 7% alcohol. One method of preparing it is as follows:

1. A good quality of grain is taken (the Nubians use wheat); the dirt is removed and the grain coarsely ground.

2. Three-quarters of the ground grain is put into a large wooden basin and kneaded with water into a dough, yeast being added.

3. The dough is made into thick loaves, which are baked lightly, so as not to destroy the enzymes.

4. The remaining quarter of grain is moistened with water and exposed to the air for some time, after which it is crushed while still moist.

A barley field. Relief from the temple of the Aten at el-Amarna; 18th Dynasty. Schimmel collection, New York.

5. The loaves are broken up and put into a vessel with water, and the crushed moist grain is added. The mixture will ferment on its own, but sometimes some old *bouza* is added.

6. After fermentation the mixture is strained through a sieve.

Diodorus said of ancient Egyptian beer that its smell and sweetness was not much inferior to wine (1.34). Sometimes a liquid made from crushed dates was added to make it even sweeter.

   Barley found use in ancient medicine. Barley porridge is today used as a poultice, and barley water is a soothing remedy for stomach disorders, although on its own it hardly had the laxative effect with which the Egyptians credited it:

A *hin* of barley, fully dried and toasted, is shaped into cakes, steeped in oil and eaten by a man who cannot get purgation. (E 37)

The effect of this remedy would lie in the kind of oil used. A remedy with barley was also believed to kill round worm:

Upper Egyptian barley 5 ro; northern salt 2½ ro; water 10 ro; remains overnight in the dew, is strained and taken for one day. (E 51)

A broken bone was treated with:

set cow's milk; flour of fresh barley 1; is combined to a paste and used as a bandage for four days. (H 219)

The white spots of a burn were bandaged with:

barley bread; oil or fat; is mixed to a paste and used as a bandage very often so that the patient gets well soon. Really excellent. (E 509)

With emmer, barley was used in a birth prognosis:

Barley and emmer. The woman must moisten it with urine every day like [she does the] dates and the sand, after it has been placed in two bags. If both grow, she will give birth. If the barley grows, it means a male child. If the emmer grows, it means a female child. If neither grows, she will not give birth. (Bln 199)

It has been suggested that the sex of the child in the prognosis was determined for linguistic reasons: the word for barley happens to be masculine, whereas that of emmer is femine. Be this as it may, it is interesting that the Egyptians had the notion that pregnancy could be detected in the woman's urine.

Hyphaene thebaica L.   *Dôm*-palm

Ancient Egyptian: tree ⸗𓆙𓅱𓆰𓐰 *m3m3*; fruit 𓐠𓃀𓐰𓃀 *ḳwḳw*

Coptic ⲃⲛⲛⲉ ⲕⲟⲩⲕ ('nut palm')

Greek κουκυφόρον

Modern Egyptian Arabic دوم *dôm*

The *dôm*-palm with its characteristic bifurcate trunk grows in Upper Egypt. The fruits are about the size of an apple, with little pulp. Inside the nut there is a sweet juice. The leaves are used for basketry and the wood for carpentry. The white nut is made into 'ivory' buttons.

Dôm-fruits are frequently found in Egyptian tombs from prehistoric times onwards. Ramesses III offered 449 and 500 measures of them to Amun-Re at Thebes. The wood was used for making boats, and the fruits were consumed. Monkeys seem to have been particularly fond of them. The astringent pulp could have found use in medicine, but there is no record of it. Theophrastus mentions that the Egyptians made bread of *dôm* to cure stomach ailments, a remedy used today, and to treat fevers (II.6.10). The inhabitants of the Sahara are known to use *dôm* for this purpose. Dioscorides also refers to the medicinal use of *dôm* (I.149).

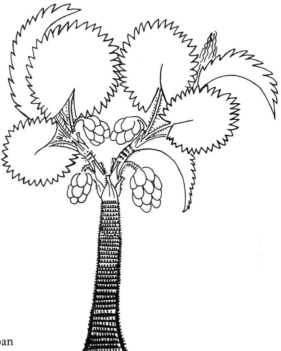

Dôm-palm. Wall-painting in Theban Tomb no. 290; Ramesside.

Inula graveolens   Inula conyza   Fleabane

Ancient Egyptian ⌐⌐ဿ *bbt*

Coptic ⲉⲛⲅ

Greek κόνυζα ἡ θήλεια

Modern Egyptian Arabic = Classical Arabic صباق *ṭabâq*
or حشيشة البراغيت *ḥašîšet el-baraġyt* ('flea grass')

Fleabane is a large perennial plant which grows wild in Europe and Asia. Two varieties are to be found in Egypt. The leaves have a very penetrating scent disagreeable to animals. It has been used as a herb for wounds and insecticide, and the stems can be burnt as a fumigant. It is strongly antibacterial.

Among the classical authors Theophrastus says that *I. conyza* drives away 'wild beasts' (VI.5.2), and Dioscorides repeats that it keeps reptiles and fleas at bay and that the Egyptians called it *keti* (III.136). Pliny states that one of the varieties (*Inula helenium*) was used as an antidote to poisons (*NH*.XX.xix). Some of these properties are reflected in pharaonic tradition. In the medical texts fleabane is, indeed, used to combat fleas:

A remedy made to expel fleas from the house: fleabane is ground with charcoal; spread it well over the house so that they go away. (E 841)

In the so-called Book of the Dead (a book on the Underworld which every Egyptian who could afford it brought with him in the tomb) fleabane is recommended to drive away crocodiles in case such a beast came one's way.

Inula helenium (elecampane) is mentioned in Apicius as a condiment for sauces and hors d'oeuvres to help digestion. Dioscorides mentions that the root, in Egyptian called *lenis* when drunk with wine helped those stung by a snake (I.27). It is nowadays candied and used to flavour sweets and liqueurs.

Juniperus phoenicea L.   *Juniperus drupacea* L.   Juniper

Ancient Egyptian 𓍿𓏤𓎡 *wꜥn*

Coptic (the resin perhaps ⲤⲒϤⲈ = Ancient Egyptian 𓊨𓈖 *sft* = Greek κεδραία = *Pinus cedrus* L.)

Greek: called 'cedar' by Herodotus and Diodorus

Modern Egyptian Arabic عرعر *ʿarʿar*

Juniper trees grow to up to 5m in height and can attain an age of several hundred years. They were probably never indigenous to Egypt proper, although a group of *J. phoenicea* actually grows in the mountains of Sinai. Most juniper timber was imported, presumably from Asia Minor, where it grew in abundance. The wood was used for carpentry, and the berries had multiple uses in medicine. The berries have an aromatic resinous flavour and are frequently used in stews, particularly to emphasise the flavour of game. The distilled oil adds its characteristic flavour to the Dutch genever. Juniper branches impart a delicate aroma to grilled food, and they were once used as a fumigant. The berries and leaves of various varieties of juniper are widely used in herbal medicine, being antiseptic, diuretic, stimulant and carminative. An infusion of the berries helps flatulence and indigestion, a secret already discovered by the ancient Egyptians. Several laxative prescriptions include the berries:

A remedy to expel purulence in the belly: notched sycamore fruits 1/8; grapes 1/16;

persea fruit(?) 1/8; figs 1/8; frankincense 1/64; cumin 1/64; juniper berries 1/16; goose fat 1/16; sweet beer 25 ro; is strained and boiled and taken for four days. (E 89)

A remedy to cause defecation: juniper berries 1; honey 1; sweet beer; is strained and drunk for four days. (H 59)

A remedy to treat tapeworm: juniper berries 5 ro; white oil 5 ro; is taken for one day. (E 85)

A remedy to treat the belly and anus: cyperus rhizomes ['tiger nuts'] 1/8; sweet beer 1/4; honey 1/16; frankincense 1/64; juniper berries 1/16; raisins 5 ro; figs 1/8; persea fruit (?) 1/8; remains overnight in the dew, is strained and taken every day. (E 137 = E 152)

Juniper berries were used as an antiseptic poultice after a suppository had caused bleeding:

juniper berries; are crushed, left in the dew and applied to the body so that the patient gets well. (B 6)

Asthma was eased by a maceration including the berries:

A remedy to eradicate asthma: figs 1/8; persea fruit (?) 1/8; grapes 1/8; notched sycamore fruits 1/8; frankincense 1/64; cumin 1/64; juniper berries 1/16; wine 2½ ro; goose fat 1/8; sweet beer 5 ro; is ground, mixed, strained and taken for four days. (E 327)

A fragrant, stimulant ointment was believed to cure headache:

A remedy for a head which is ill to kill the pain: frankincense 1; cumin 1; juniper berries 1; goose fat 1; to be boiled and the head is anointed therewith. (E 254)

An infusion in milk of juniper berries, cumin, frankincense and an unidentified pod along with bone marrow was given to a woman who had not been

Picking juniper berries. Relief in the tomb of Niankhkhnum and Khnumhotep at Saqqara; Old Kingdom.

menstruating for several years (E 833). Interestingly, it was also used in a vaginal suppository to induce childbirth, mixed with fir resin and an unidentified plant (E 806). In modern herbal medicine it is contraindicated in pregnancy.

The use of juniper oil can be traced back through history. Prospero Alpini says that it was used to massage the body before an attack of fever was expected. Afterwards, when the patient had been made to perspire, he was covered up to increase the effect. It was also used for children if smallpox was suspected (*Médicine*, 318). In ancient Egypt an oil scented with essential oil of juniper was used in mummification to anoint the corpse. The berries have been shown to have been mixed with the salt in which the bodies were laid for dehydration, at least among the early Christians: 'In Nubia, in a cemetery thought to be about the 5th century AD, the bodies were packed in large quantities of salt, mixed in some instances with the same kind of small globular fruit or berries already mentioned' (Lucas, *Anc. Eg. Mat.*, p. 311); the berries are undoubtedly juniper. The monks in a Coptic monastery at Thebes had also been buried in salt and juniper berries: 'The body was . . . laid on the first grave sheet and handfuls of coarse rock salt and juniper berries were placed between the legs and over the trunk inside and outside the innermost wrappings' (Lucas, *ibid.*, quoting Winlock). When discussing 'cedar' Dioscorides adds that 'it is a preservative of dead [bodies], hence some have called it "the life of him that is dead"' (1.105).

Sawdust and wood pitch of juniper have also been found on pharaonic mummies. Sawdust was one of the ingredients in a refreshing poultice which included various resins, wax, coriander, pork fat and ox fat (E 652 = H 101). The twigs of juniper were added to a prescription for a patient suffering from illness in the head and neck. It consisted of ladanum, frankincense, *kohl*, red ochre, ibex fat and an unidentified balm, to be grated and made into a bandage (E 298).

There is evidence of juniper having been used for dyeing in ancient times. A text tells that 'fresh juniper' was employed to dye a strip of linen used in the cult at the temple of Dendara in Upper Egypt. When mordanted with alum or chrome juniper berries produce a pale creamy-brown dye.

Lactuca sativa L.   *Lactuca virosa* L.   Lettuce

Ancient Egyptian: *L. sativa* ⸗ 𓂝𓃀𓅱 *ʿbw*; presumably *L. virosa* 𓇋𓆑 *ỉft*

Coptic ϣϥ

Greek θρῖδαξ

Modern Egyptian Arabic خس *ḥass*

Lactuca sativa is the variety known in Britain as Cos lettuce, in France as 'romaine'. It is also widely eaten in modern Egypt. An oil can be extracted from the seeds.

Cutting and watering lettuces and onions. Relief in the tomb of Niankhkhnum and Khnumhotep at Saqqara; Old Kingdom.

In the Assyrian Herbal the seeds were used with cumin as an eye poultice (§ 10 CN). Dioscorides says that the Egyptians called the plant *embrosi* (II.165). The latex of the older variety of *L. sativa* was used as a cough suppressant and mild sedative, and even as an anti-aphrodisiac. In ancient Egypt the plant had the opposite connotations. It was sacred to Min, god of fertility, because of its milky juice, reminiscent of semen. It was also related to the god Seth in an erotic context: he became pregnant after eating lettuces on which had been scattered the semen of his rival, the god Horus. Specimens of lettuce seed have been found, and the plant is frequently represented on the monuments. The priests in the temple of Philae were not allowed to eat lettuce.

The word ʿ*bw* is conspicuously absent from the medical texts, but it has recently been suggested that ʿ*ft*, hitherto translated 'melilot', is indeed the designation for *L. virosa*. In that case the Egyptians used it for a number of purposes:

A remedy to treat illness in one half of the belly: ʿ*ft* 1; date juice 1; boil in oil or fat and use as a poultice. (E 40)

A remedy to remove pain in the belly: fresh beef 5 ro; frankincense 1/64; ʿ*ft* 1/8; juniper berries 1/16; fresh bread 1/8; sweet beer 25 ro; is strained and drunk for four days. (E 86)

A remedy to expel worm from the belly: ʿ*ft* 1; chaste tree 1; fermented plant juice 1; is combined and eaten. Afterwards the patient will relieve himself of all the worms in his belly. (E 64)

Treatment of any ailment from which a patient might suffer, that is any purulence: Lower Egyptian salt 1; ʿ*ft* 1; is ground in oil or fat and used as a poultice. (E 530)

A remedy to treat purulence in the ears: ʿ*ft*: ʿ*ft* is mixed with ladanum and poured into the ear. (Bln 301)

Chopped ʿ*ft* was thought to encourage the growth of hair if applied (E 467). Boiled with other ingredients, such as fermented plant juice, oil, beer, ʿ*ft* and another plant, it was used to soothe a cough when strained and drunk for four days (E 312). Finally, it was used in a general pain-killing beverage and another laxative concoction, as well as in medicine taken for eye complaints.

The Copts used the seeds of lettuce ground with warm water as a worm-killing beverage (Ch 111). The latex of a bitter lettuce, mixed with honey and opium, was used to treat the eyes (Ch 8).

Lawsonia inermis L.   Henna

Ancient Egyptian 𓈖𓏌𓏲 *ḥnw*(?)
Coptic ⲕⲟⲩⲡⲉⲣ
Greek κύπρος
Modern Egyptian Arabic ﺣﻨﺎ *ḥinna*

The shrub, which can grow as tall as 6m, probably originated somewhere in Persia and now grows in Egypt and the Middle East. Dioscorides claims that in his days the henna grown at Canopus in the Delta was among the best (I.124). Its pink or cream-coloured flowers have a sweet scent and produce blue-black berries. The dried powdered leaves are cooling and astringent, and are extensively used as a hair dye, occasionally also for dyeing cloth. In Nubia the leaves are placed in the hollows of the arms as a deodorant, and the dark-skinned women use it for dyeing their bodies, with the result that they acquire the colour of a ripe date. They also use it mixed with acacia leaves for rubbing sore hands and feet. In Islamic medicine henna with vinegar applied to the head is believed to cure headaches and other pains caused by excess heat. Burns and blisters are also found to benefit from treatment with henna. Alpini quotes henna powder to treat sore and evil-smelling feet and as a general deodorant (*Plantes*, p. 46).

The leaves have been found in tombs of the Late Period and of Ptolemaic date, but the actual use of the plant as a colouring agent is somewhat disputed. Although there is evidence that the Egyptians coloured their finger-nails, there is no proof that they used henna to do so. Some mummies were found to have their hair dyed red, and henna may have been used for this. The Romans certainly used the plant for this purpose, as do women in Islamic countries today.

Pliny mentions an Egyptian unguent made from *Cyprinum*, an Egyptian tree which was probably henna (*NH*.XII.li). A tentative identification of *ḥnw* for henna has been suggested. It occurs in a prescription where the stimulant properties of the herb would be useful:

A remedy to cure an ailment which causes loss of hair: flax; *ḥnw*-plant; is boiled and steeped in oil with fly dung. Grind to a paste and apply. (E 774)

The word 𓂝𓈖𓐍𓇌𓏌 *ʿnḫ-imy* has also been suggested for henna. The scent of this herb was reputed to resurrect the dead man or woman who sniffed it. It is used in a bandage to treat a tumour:

ʿnḫ-imy 1; salt 1; honey; is ground finely and applied. (Bln 53)

Lens culinaris Medic (syn. *Lens esculenta* Moench)   Lentils

Ancient Egyptian ⸗⸗⸗⸗⸗⸗ '*3rš3n*

Coptic ⲁⲣϣⲓⲛ

Greek φακός

Modern Egyptian Arabic عدس '*ads*

Lentils are known to have been part of the diet in pharaonic times, but there is no record of their use for any other purpose. A basket of lentils was deposited in the tomb of Tutankhamun. Lentil dishes appear to have been particularly popular in Alexandria if we are to believe Athenaeus: 'You men of Alexandria have been brought up on lentil food, and your entire city is full of lentil dishes'. (IV.158.D)

In the Bible instructions were given for making bread from a mixture of barley, wheat, beans, lentils, millet and spelt (Ezekiel 4:9). Prospero Alpini tells how the Egyptians of his day when performing cauterisation sprinkled the wound with ground black lentils before bandaging (*Médicine*, 138).

Lepidum sativum L.   Cress

Ancient Egyptian ⸗⸗⸗⸗ *smt*

Coptic ⲕⲁⲣⲧⲁⲙⲟⲛ; ϣⲓⲧⲣⲁϭ ⲍⲛⲧⲓ; seeds ϣⲁⲉⲓⲛ

Greek κάρδαμον

Modern Egyptian Arabic رشاد *rešâd* or حرف *ḥurf*

Cress is a tall herb with white flowers and a pod 5cm long. It grows wild, and is cultivated in Egypt today for use as a stimulant and diuretic, and in poultices. Prospero Alpini lists cress (seeds) as one of several ingredients in a mixture of herbs and spices in honey used to cure catarrh, but the remedy was believed to be beneficial for mind and body in general (*Médicine*, 311).

Cress seeds were found in the tomb of Kha, but there is no mention of them in pharaonic medical texts under the name of *smt*. It is probably to be found among the several unidentified seeds. The Copts used cress for headache:

frankincense 1 drachme; cress 1 drachme; [is mixed] with the white of an egg and applied. (Ch 63)

Runny eyes were treated with a mixture of blood and cress (Ryl 7). It was also taken with other ingredients as a laxative to expel fever (Ryl 5).

Ancient Egyptian 〰𓈖𓏏𓏥 *mhy*

Coptic: seeds ⲉϥⲣⲁ ⲙⲁⲍⲉ; also ⲑⲉⲣϣ ('red coloured')

Greek: plant λίνον; seeds λινόσπερμον

Modern Egyptian Arabic: plant كتّان *kittân*; seeds بزر الكتّان *bizr el-kittân*

This well-known annual is cultivated for its stems, which are used in the manufacture of linen, and for its seeds, which produce linseed oil. This latter is now used as a paint oil because it is fast drying. This was not the case in pharaonic times, where pigments were mixed with other ingredients. In medicine linseed was formerly used as a laxative, but it is now considered to be unsafe. The seeds are still added to certain types of bread in Scandinavia and Germany. In present-day Egypt the oil is used by the poorer people in the Egyptian national dish *fôl medammes* (beans); others substitute olive oil. It is also employed as a lamp oil. It has the disadvantage of going rancid very quickly.

Flax was grown from a very early date in Egypt, as finds of the fibres show. The earliest record of linseed oil dates from the Ptolemaic period, but the oil was undoubtedly in use much earlier as a cooking and lamp oil. In medicine it appears only to have been used externally. Leaves of flax, cyperus grass, a liquid and an unidentified ingredient were made into a suppository to treat swelling at the anus (haemorrhoids?), and 'heat' in the belly was eased with:

capsules of the tips of flax 1; fermented plant juice; is placed on the belly of the man who suffers. (E 179)

A bandage for the nails of the fingers or toes was made of ochre, linseed, an unidentified part of the sycamore fig, honey and oil or fat (H 187). A poultice of the seeds does indeed relieve pain and heals skin wounds and suppurations. Prospero Alpini lists linseed as one of the ingredients added to a basic preparation to be taken as a pain-killer (*Médicine*, 266). Linseed is mentioned only once in Coptic prescriptions to treat an illness called *sir*: linseed, figs, gum and honey are given to the patient to eat, 'but he must drink fig juice afterwards' (Ch 22).

Pulling flax in the Underworld. Wall-painting in Theban Tomb no. 1; 19th Dynasty.

Malus sylvestris Mill. Apple

Ancient Egyptian 𓏠𓏭𓊪𓈖 or 𓄿𓇋𓀀 *dph*
Coptic ⲭⲉⲙⲡⲉⳍ
Greek μηλέα
Modern Egyptian Arabic تفاح *tiffâḥ*

The apple is too well known to require any description. In the Bible it is known as *tappuaḥ*, and it is mentioned by classical authors as for example Theophrastus, Pliny and Dioscorides. Prospero Alpini mentions it as part of the Egyptian diet (*Médicine*, 252), but the Egyptian climate was never perfect for cultivating apples. They remain a luxury and are largely imported. Ramesses II had apple trees planted in his garden in the Delta, and Ramesses III claims to have offered 848 baskets of the fruit to Hapy, god of the Nile and fertility.

The tree and fruit do not seem to have been used in Egyptian medicine. In the Assyrian Herbal, however, under the name *ḥašḥuru* it is used to treat a venereal disease. It should be said though that in antiquity there seemed to be some confusion between 'apple' and 'apricot'.

The variety of apples nowadays bears witness to the popularity and usefulness of the fruit. Among the varieties available one (Court Pendu Plat) is said to have been grown since Roman times.

Mandragora officinarum L. Mandrake

Ancient Egyptian 𓇌𓐍𓂝𓏤 *rrmt*
Coptic ⲛⲟⲩⲧⲉⲙ (?)
Greek μανδραγόρας
Modern Egyptian Arabic يابروة *jabrûh*

Mandrake is a perennial, almost stemless, plant on a thick root, with long leaves and greenish-yellow or purplish flowers and orange, fleshy many-seeded fruit. It grows wild in warm climates. It is a poisonous plant connected with mysticism and magic through the ages.
It came to Egypt some time during the New Kingdom.

Lotus, mandrake and poppy(?) held by Tutankhamun. Scene incised on the king's golden shrine; 18th Dynasty. Egyptian Museum, Cairo.

Picking mandrake fruits at el-Amarna. From the ivory casket of Tutankhamun. Egyptian Museum, Cairo.

No remains of an actual plant have as yet been found. Dioscorides claims that the Egyptians called the plant *aperioum* (IV.76).

Although the word *rrmt* does not occur in the pharaonic medical texts, it is more than likely that the plant was available for medicinal purposes. The leaves were formerly used externally for ulcers, and the root as a pain-killer, narcotic and aphrodisiac. To gain some idea of the importance of mandrake in the ancient world one may quote the following paragraphs from Theophrastus: 'It is said that one should draw three circles round mandrake with a sword and cut it with one's face towards the west; and at the cutting of the second piece one should dance round the plant and say as many things as possible about the

A gardener at work. In the lower right-hand corner is a mandrake; the other plants include a pomegranate, a willow, cornflowers, papyrus and lotus flowers. Wall-painting in Theban Tomb no. 217; Ramesside.

mysteries of love . . . The leaf of this mandrake, used with meal, is useful for wounds, and the root for erysipelas, when scraped and steeped in vinegar, and also for gout, for sleeplessness, and for love potions. It is administered in wine or vinegar; they cut little balls of it as of radishes, and making a string of them hang them up in the smoke over must' (IX.8.8; IX.9.1).

The fruit appears to have had a symbolic erotic significance in pharaonic times. It also frequently occurs in Egyptian ornaments, but it is sometimes difficult to distinguish it from the rather similarly rendered persea fruit.

Our word 'mandrake' appears to be derived from Sumerian NAM-TAR ('plague god plant'). In their herbals both root, leaf, seed and juice are used medicinally for toothache, as a stomachic, and for rubbing on a woman in labour (§ 51).

Medemia argun Württemb. ex Mart.   *Argûn*-palm

Ancient Egyptian 𓄿𓄿𓈖𓊪𓈖𓏏𓆱 *m3m3- n-ḥ3nn*
Coptic ?
Greek ?
Modern Egyptian Arabic عرجون *argûn*

The *argûn* is a fan palm like the *dôm*-palm but its stem is unbranched. It has an ellipsoid edible fruit about 4cm in length which is a deep-purple colour with yellow flesh. The tree now grows sparsely in the Sudan. In ancient Egypt it was a garden tree. Ineni, the builder, tells with pride that he had a specimen planted in his garden about 1510 BC. Fruits of *argûn* have been found in burials of 5th Dynasty date.

Melilotus officinalis L.   Yellow sweet clover (Melilot)

Ancient Egyptian ?
Coptic ΜΕΛΙΛΙΤΟΝ
Greek μελίλωτος
Modern Egyptian Arabic اكايل الملك *aklîl el-malik*

This plant grows wild in Europe, Asia and the USA, and is widely used as fodder. The flowering tops contain coumarin with a strong sweet almond smell, which is released on drying. It is used to flavour certain dishes, as for example sausages, marinades and beer, and also tobacco. The herb was formerly used to treat a number of different conditions, being carminative, expectorant, antithrombotic and antibiotic. Sweet clover tea is believed to help digestion. The flowers attract bees, but repel moths. It has been used as a strewing herb. The leaves can be eaten as a vegetable, but they are rather bitter.

Prospero Alpini refers to melilot as a 'warming' herb (*Médicine*, 253), used with others in a poultice to treat fever (*Médicine*, 318), the seeds being added to a basic beverage to ease pain (*Médicine*, 266).

The ancient Egyptian word for melilot was believed to be ʿft, but this word has recently been shown to be more likely to refer to lettuce, in which case we have not yet identified a word for melilot in the pharaonic medical texts. A Coptic medical papyrus mentions melilot in a prescription to treat sick testicles:

melilot, rose, 'bride's wreath'; grind it; let the patient drink it with wine. With the help of God he will recover. (Ch 171)

Mentha piperita L.   Peppermint

Ancient Egyptian ? (see below)

Coptic ?

Greek ? (names exist for other varieties)

Modern Egyptian Arabic نعناع *naʿnaʿ*

The place of origin of this well known perennial is unknown, but it is now cultivated in Egyptian gardens, as it was in ancient times. In a tomb dating from the Late Period part of a bouquet was found, including the leaves of peppermint. Its ancient name has not yet been identified with certainty, and its use in medicine remains obscure. Dioscorides mentions an Egyptian name for mint as *tis* (III.41); this has been identified as *Mentha sativa* (also an ingredient in *kyphi*; see under Perfumes above).

Nowadays peppermint is used to treat flatulence, as a digestive and antiseptic, and for toothache and colds. The essential oil contains menthol. In the days of Apicius it was widely used in cooking. In England it is also the traditional accompaniment to lamb, whereas in the Middle East it flavours yoghurt and honey, and it is widely used for a tea. Liqueurs and confectionery also benefit from the characteristic aroma of the herb. Prospero Alpini recalls that to treat fever a warm decoction of mint was administered to the patient before the attack, but with the unsavoury addition of a little ground snakeskin (*Médicine*, 320).

Mimusops laurifolius (Forsk.) Friis
syn. *schimperi* A. Rich

Persea

Ancient Egyptian 𓈝𓅓𓎼𓃀𓊪𓏤 *š3w3b*

Coptic ϢⲂⲈ; ϢⲞⲨⲈ

Greek περσέα

Modern Egyptian Arabic = Classical Arabic لبخ *labaḫ*, although this now designates *Albizzia lebbekh* Bth, a tree imported from India in the 18th century

Persea is a tall tree with a dense foliage of tough leaves. The fruits are about 4cm long, round with a pointed tip and four or six sepals. When ripe it is yellow and contains a sweet, green edible pulp enclosing two or three stones. The tree grows wild in Ethiopia, and in ancient times it grew all over Egypt. Fruits have been found in burials of the Old Kingdom and later, and leaves have been identified in mummy garlands from the New Kingdom, where they formed the basis for the setting of other floral elements. The fruit occurs frequently in representations, though it is sometimes difficult to distinguish from the fruit of the mandrake. The sepals of persea are generally shorter than those of mandrake. In the Roman period the tree was dying out in Egypt, and cutting was prohibited. By the seventeenth century it had completely disappeared. Only at the beginning of the present century has it been re-introduced into Egyptian gardens.

The classical authors frequently mention the tree which, they say, only grew in Egypt: '... In Egypt, there is another tree called the persea, which in

Picking *išd*: this word is generally interpreted as persea. Relief from a tomb at Memphis; 5th Dynasty. Ägyptisches Museum, West Berlin (Inv. Nr. 3/65).

Persea bouquet from the tomb of Tutankhamun; 18th Dynasty.

appearance is large and fair, and it almost resembles a pear in leaves, flowers, branches, and general form, but it is evergreen . . . It bears abundant fruit and at every season, for the new fruit always overtakes that of last year. It ripens as fruit at the season of the etesian winds; the other fruit they gather somewhat unripe and store it. In size it is as large as a pear, but in shape it is oblong, almond-shaped, and its colour is grass-green. It has inside a stone like a plum, but much smaller and softer; the flesh is sweet and luscious and easily digested; for it does not hurt if one eats it in quantity' (Theophrastus VI.2.5).

In pharaonic Egypt the persea was a favourite garden tree, and both the fruit and the branches were used for decoration, the fruit presumably being consumed as well. Two large bouquets were found in the tomb of Tutankhamun. In the medical texts it occurs just once in a remedy for 'white spots', an ointment consisting of red ochre, *kohl*, boiled persea pulp, and another plant ingredient, pounded in sycamore juice (L 57). It is possible that the fruit is disguised under another name, as yet unidentified, in other medical prescriptions. The word 𓊹𓎼𓏤 *išd* is generally taken to designate the persea tree and its fruit, used frequently in texts of non-medical nature.

Moringa pterygosperma   *Moringa aptera*   Moringa

Ancient Egyptian: oil 𓃀𓄿𓎡 *b3ḳ*

Coptic ?

Greek βαλανος μυρεφική

Modern Egyptian Arabic بان *ban* or يسار *jasâr*

Moringa is a tall tree, carrying pods with nut-like seeds of a bitter-sweet taste (behen nuts). *M. pterygosperma* is indigenous to Egypt and still grows there. The oil (ben oil) is odourless, yellowish and with a sweet taste. It is favoured for cosmetics, as it does not easily go rancid, and it is also used for cooking. It was extensively used in pharaonic medicine either on its own or as a vehicle, frequently with honey, for remedies incorporating other ingredients.

A remedy for the stomach: honey 1; moringa oil 1; frankincense 1; wine 1; is combined to a paste, boiled and eaten. (E 214)

What is done for someone who has cramps(?) as a result of a wound: barley flour 1; ox fat 1; moringa oil 1; boil it, and let the patient eat it, even if he does not want to. (E 526)

To ease pain in the anus an enema was resorted to:

honey 2½ ro; moringa oil 1/4; sweet beer 10 ro; use as an enema for four days. (Bln 163h)

Honey 5 ro; moringa oil 5 ro; fermented plant juice 20 ro; Lower Egyptian salt 1/16; use as an enema for four days. (Bln 164b)

A remedy for pain in the stomach: moringa oil 1/4; fermented plant juice 7½ ro; use as an enema for four days. (Bln 170)

If a patient suffered from sore gums which were being eaten away, a masticatory was recommended, mixed of moringa oil, gum, figs, water, ochre and four unidentified plants (E 747). To cure illness in the head a soothing unguent was prepared:

castor oil seeds 1; fat 1; moringa oil; is made into a paste and used every day. (E 437)

A refreshing ointment included:

moringa oil; Lower Egyptian salt; ibex fat; frankincense; cyperus grass; is ground finely to a paste and applied. (Bln 102)

Blood was removed, that is to say stopped, from a wound by applying a poultice of:

wax 1; fat 1; moringa oil 1; honey 1; carob pod pulp(?) 1; boiled barley 1; is boiled, combined and the wound bandaged for four days. (E 517)

Ear drops were mixed of:

moringa oil 1; ochre 1; cucumber 1. (Bln 202)

Moringa oil, when applied to the skin, was thought to prevent mosquitoes from stinging (E 846).

Myrtus communis L. — Myrtle

Ancient Egyptian 𓎛𓏏� *ḥt–ds*(?)

Coptic?

Greek μυρσίνη or μυρρίνη

Modern Egyptian Arabic آس *âs*

Myrtle is an aromatic evergreen shrub with glossy dark-green leaves, white fragrant flowers and later bluish berries. It is native to the Mediterranean, and it now grows there wild and cultivated. The fresh or dried leaves, flowers and fruit are astringent and antiseptic and are used as a condiment and in cosmetics. In classical times it was the plant of Venus, goddess of love, and a bride would wear it on her wedding day, a custom which still prevails. A wreath including myrtle and a spray of the leaves of ancient date has been found. The word *ḥt-ds* has been suggested for myrtle. If this is correct, there is ample reference to it in the medical texts. It is often an ingredient in mixed herbs used for fumigation. Once it occurs on its own for that purpose to treat a nervous disease(?) in the face:

ḥt-ds; the man is to be fumigated with it; quench it with sweet beer so that he begins to perspire. Massage him with your hand. (Bln 76)

It was prescribed for urinary disorders:

ḥt-ds 1; grind in fermented plant juice and apply to the male member. (E 269)

Other external applications included the following:

A remedy to remove mucus when you suffer from it on the right or left side of the chest: *ḥt-ds*; porridge; apply as a bandage for four days. (Bln 142)

Another remedy [to remove mucus if you suffer from it in any part of the body during the winter]: zizyphus leaves 5 ro; *ḥt-ds*-leaves 5 ro; porridge 1/4; ox fat 2½ ro; sawdust of fir 5 ro; apply as a bandage. (Bln 141)

Another remedy to treat pain: wheatmeal 1; barley flour 1; emmer flour 1; *ḥt-ds* 1; honey 1; apply as a bandage. (E 129)

A remedy to treat heat in the stomach: emmer grains 1; boiled wheat 1; boiled wheatmeal 1; barley flour 1; *ḥt-ds* 1; honey 1; apply as a bandage to the abdomen. (E 175)

To treat swelling: beans; *ḥt-ds*; dregs of beer; persea(?) fruit; wax; combine to a paste and apply as a bandage for four days. (H 137)

A remedy to treat stiffness in any limb: *ḥt-ds*; ox fat 1; beans 1; frankincense 1; apply as a bandage. (E 672)

The herb was taken internally to treat a cough:

Fermented plant juice 1/4; oil or fat 1/4; beer 1/4; is placed in a pot and boiled. Grind ʿft-lettuce, *ḥt-ds* and add to the pot; when it has boiled and strained give it (to the patient) to drink for four days. (E 312)

Another remedy to soothe a cough: ʿft-lettuce 1; sweet beer 1; oil or fat 1; ḫt-ds 1; fermented plant juice 1; combine [and give to the patient to drink] for four days. (Bln 36)

Finally, a hair ointment was prepared from a red mineral, kohl, ḫt-ds, oil or fat; gazelle dung and hippopotamus fat (E 471).

In Coptic medicine essential oil of myrtle was used in a prescription with fresh rue and a mineral for a number of skin ailments (Ch 219). Dioscorides described the preparation of the oil, saying that the leaves were steeped in olive oil so that the latter absorbed the fragrant oil contained in the leaves (I.48). The leaves and fruit had multiple uses in medicine (I.155). Pliny informs us that the myrtle with the most powerful scent grew in Egypt (NH.xv.xxxvii). The same had been claimed by Theophrastus who says that in that country it was marvellously fragrant (II.8.5) and that the berries tasted like wine. The Assyrian Herbal prescribed myrtle for fumigation, poultices and beverages and thus agrees with the Egyptian use of the herb (§ 32). Prospero Alpini quotes myrtle syrup as being taken by sick and sound alike (Médicine, 268) and myrtle oil used in an astringent enema (Médicine, 313).

Nigella sativa L.   Black cumin

Ancient Egyptian ?

Coptic ⲥⲧⲓⲕⲓⲙⲙⲉ ('black scent')

Greek μελάνθιον

Modern Egyptian Arabic: plant شونيز; šûnîz; seeds كمون أسود kamûn eswid ('black cumin') or حبة سوداء ḥabb sôda ('black seed')

The spicy seeds of this plant are used in India and other eastern countries to encourage lactation and to improve the shape of the breasts. It is also used to flavour bread and other dishes. Remains of the plant were found in the tomb of Tutankhamun, but as long as the ancient name remains unknown, the purpose for which it was used remains uncertain. The plant was mentioned in the Bible and in the Assyrian Herbal ('black TIN-TIR') as a remedy for ears, eyes and mouth, and when taken, for the stomach (§ 10 M). The Copts included the seeds in a remedy for itching skin:

Take garlic, black cumin, natron, mature vinegar, fir resin, radish oil. Boil it and use as an ointment. The skin will come off. After three days wash with warm water. (ZB 26)

Prospero Alpini quotes a similar remedy consisting of black cumin and vinegar to treat skin ailments. The seeds were used as a vermifuge for children (Plantes, 129).

Nymphaea lotus L.   White lotus

Ancient Egyptian ⌐ ᔕ *ssn*

Coptic ⲩⲱⲩⲉⲛ

Greek λωτός

Modern Egyptian Arabic بشنين أبيض *bašnyn abyaḍ* ('white lotus')
or نيلوفر *nîlûfar*

The white lotus, one of the most beloved plants in ancient Egypt, can still be found in the canals of the country. Along with blue lotus, *Nymphaea caerulea*, it was frequently represented in Egyptian art and was almost synonymous with life. The flowers and leaves of this most attractive flower did not escape the fate of all that grows, namely to become part of remedies prescribed for various ailments, among others a liver disease which may have been jaundice:

A remedy to treat the liver: lotus leaves 1/8; wine 20 ro; powdered zizyphus 1/8; figs 1/8; milk 1/16; juniper berries 1/16; frankincense 1/64; sweet beer 20 ro; is left in the dew overnight, strained and drunk for four days. (E 479)

The flowers were used in an unguent or poultice for the head with cumin, asafoetida resin(?), myrrh, moringa oil, juniper berries and an unidentified ingredient (E 258), and a demonic constipation was driven out by a potion containing lotus leaves among other ingredients (E 209). A composite liquid used as an enema also included lotus leaves (B 13b). A hair remedy, incon-

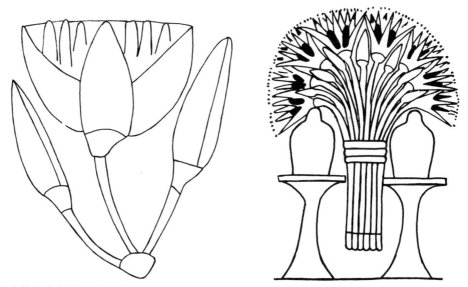

(*Above left*) *Nymphaea lotus*. Wall-painting in Theban Tomb no. 217; Ramesside.
(*Above right*) Large bouquet of lotus flowers. Wall-painting from a Theban Tomb; 18th Dynasty. Ägyptisches Museum, East Berlin, 18532.

(*Above left*) Lotus bouquet. Wall-painting in Theban Tomb no. 217; Ramesside.
(*Above right*) A lady with lotus flowers. Wall-painting in Theban Tomb no. 161, after drawing by Hay; 18th Dynasty. British Library (Hay MSS 29851, 6–7).

spicuous at first, opens up grim prospects when one reads the recommended use of it:

A remedy to cause the hair to fall out: lotus leaves, boiled and steeped in oil or fat. To be placed on the head of a hated woman. (E 475)

Lotus flowers decorated the offering tables of the gods, and large quantities were presented to them. One record mentions that no fewer than 3,410 bouquets had been given by Ramesses III to the temple of Amun.

Dioscorides tells that the root of the Egyptian lotus was eaten both raw and cooked (in the latter state it had the consistency of eggyolk), and that the seeds were used in bread (IV.114) (see above under 'In the kitchen'). Prospero Alpini tells that the Egyptians of his time considered lotus (*nenufar*) a 'cooling' herb. To bring down a temperature a patient would be immersed in a lukewarm bath scented with lotus (*Médicine*, 246); or he was left in a warm room to bring about perspiration, after which he was anointed with lotus oil, plunged in the lukewarm bath, dried off and then left to sleep before being served a light meal (*Médicine*, 248). Lotus had a cooling effect in an enema (*Médicine*, 313), especially the oil of the flower (*Médicine*, 316).

In Europe a related variety, *Nymphaea alba* L., was once taken to reduce libido. In Egypt the connotations were the opposite. *Nymphaea lotus* is sold by Egyptian herbalists for its refreshing and calming effect. The leaves and flowers of some members of the *Nymphaea* species are said to have narcotic properties.

Ocimum basilicum L.   Basil

Ancient Egyptian ?

Coptic ?

Greek (probably this variety) ὤκιμον

Modern Egyptian Arabic ريحان *ryhân*

As the name of basil has not been identified in Egyptian texts its use remains obscure, but recent finds show that the herb was known in pharaonic times. It is indigenous to India and is now grown in all the Mediterranean countries. It is an annual herb with a pungent aromatic flavour. It is widely used in cooking and is the predominant ingredient in pesto sauce. The leaves are tonic, antiseptic and digestive and are said to relieve nausea. Basil oil rubbed on the temples eases headache. It has the reputation of being aphrodisiac and was formerly used to aid childbirth. Sprinkled on the floor it leaves an aromatic scent in a room, and a pot on the window sill keeps flies away. The dried and powdered leaf has been taken as snuff. It is thus a herb with multiple uses, which cannot have failed to be recognised in ancient Egypt.

The classical writers mention basil, the 'royal' herb, as being used to flavour food and as decoration in floral garlands. Prospero Alpini lists it as one of several ingredients in a remedy to avoid contracting the plague (*Médicine*, 323).

Olea europaea L.   Olive

Ancient Egyptian 𓂧𓂧𓏏𓅱 *ḏdtw*

Coptic: tree ⲭⲟⲉⲓⲧ; oil ⲛⲉϩ ⲙⲙⲉ ('true oil')

Greek ἐλάα

Modern Egyptian Arabic زيت *zêt*

The olive tree probably originated in Asia Minor. It is mentioned in texts from Ebla dated about 2500 BC (called *giš-i-giš*) at which time the tree was already extensively cultivated. The first finds in Egypt date from the 18th Dynasty (*c.* 1350 BC), but the tree may not actually have been planted there until a later date. Theophrastus said that it grew in Upper Egypt, and that the oil produced in his days was not inferior to the Greek oil he knew, except that it had a less pleasing smell (IV.2.7). Strabo, who travelled in Egypt nearly five hundred years later, says that the trees grew only in the Fayum Oasis (XVII.1.35). It still grows there as well as in the Siwa Oasis further west. To grow successfully, the tree needs more rain than it would receive in Upper Egypt today.

In the New Kingdom the olives and the oil were imported, first from Syria and later from Greece. When the tree came to grow in Egypt the leaves were used for decorative purposes. A large bouquet of persea twigs from the tomb of Tutankhamun had a few olive twigs inserted, and three wreaths from the same tomb were partly composed of olive leaves. A bouquet of a later date recently found consisted of olive and *Origanum majorana*.

Ramesses III attempted to plant an olive grove near the temple of the sun-god Re at Heliopolis: 'I planted olive groves for you in your town, Heliopolis, equipped with many people who make pure oil, first class from Egypt, in order to light the lamps in your holy dwelling'.

Apart from being used as lamp oil, the precious fluid would have been consumed, and used for steeping flowers to make fragrant oils. There is no indication of it having been used for medicinal purposes. Among the Copts 'true oil', that is to say olive oil, was used as a vehicle for various remedies, mainly unguents and poultices and rarely in drugs to be taken.

Olive branches for the Aten.
Relief from the temple of the
Aten, el-Amarna; 18th Dynasty.
Schimmel collection, New York.

Origanum majorana L.   Sweet marjoram

Ancient Egyptian ?

Coptic ⲟⲣⲓⲕⲁⲛⲟⲛ

Greek ἀμάϱαϰον

Modern Egyptian Arabic بردقوش *bardaqôš* or مردقوش *mardaqôš*

The ancient Egyptian name of this herb native to the Mediterranean has not yet been identified with any certainty, but both Dioscorides (III.47) and Pliny (*NH*.XXI.xxxv) claim that the Egyptian name for the herb was *sopho* or *samp-suchum*, that is to say 'herb of the god Sobek' (see above, under 'Perfume').

Dioscorides even gives the name of an oil of marjoram as 'sampsuchinon' (I.58). The plant has been found in mummy garlands dating from the first century AD. It must have been a common herb in Egyptian gardens then, as it is today.

In Coptic medicine 'origanum' is prescribed for a sick ear:

origanum; hyssop; boil it well and apply. (Ch 173)

Prospero Alpini refers to marjoram as a 'warming' herb (*Médicine*, 253). Theophrastus says that sweet marjoram was used in perfumery (IX.7.3). This is one of its many uses during the centuries. It is also antiseptic, tonic and digestive, and marjoram tea was thought to cure a cold, soothe the nerves and provoke menstruation. Rubbed into the skin, the herb would ease rheumatism and headaches, and chewing the leaves would soothe toothache. The leaves are used for strewing on floors, and they lend a delicate flavour to many cooked dishes and salads, often being replaced by other varieties of the herb.

Papaver somniferum L.   Common poppy

Ancient Egyptian 〰 *špn* (?)

Coptic ?

Greek μήκων (ἡ ὀπώδης)

Modern Egyptian Arabic: flower أبو النوم *abû en-nôm* ('father of sleep') or خشخاش *hošhâš*; juice افيون *afiûn* (opium)

This pink poppy is cultivated as a drug crop in some countries, including Egypt. The main constituent in the plant, particularly in the latex, is morphine. It acts as an analgesic, narcotic, stimulant and euphoric. In the classical world it was used as a sedative. Overdoses are fatal.

Red poppies.
Wall-painting in
Theban Tomb no. 1;
19th Dynasty.

Prospero Alpini explained the use and effect of opium in Egypt in his time: it stimulates men in war and in love, and causes spectacular dreams. But although the Egyptians had become used to taking large quantities, there were side effects, for the users became comatose, lethargic and inconsistent. The best opium came from a locality called 'Sajeth' (Said = Upper Egypt) which he identifies as the location of ancient Thebes (*Médicine*, 255, 261).

In ancient Egypt *špn*, very dubiously identified as poppy, was used to produce beer, and *špn* occurs occasionally in medical texts:

A remedy for too much crying in a child: *špn*-seeds; fly dung from the wall; is made to a paste, [mixed with water?], strained and drunk for four days. The crying will cease instantly. (E 782)

The seeds of *špn* were part of an unguent:

Boiled hippopotamus skin 1; oil or fat 1; *špn*-seeds 1; carob pod pulp(?) 1; is combined to a paste and used as a unguent. (E 443)

With the addition of a mineral, myrrh and chalcedon *špn*-seeds were ground to a powder for an external remedy (E 445). In more recent herbal medicine poppy is applied to bruised or inflamed skin. In Egypt it is mixed with spices and eaten or smoked. It is commonly believed to be an aphrodisiac.

The species *Papaver rhoeas* L. was also known in ancient Egypt and with its bright red petals it was frequently depicted as an ornamental flower. Dioscorides quotes the same Egyptian name for both, *nanti* (IV.64). In modern herbal medicine these flowers are used as a sedative and for colic and coughs.

Among the many items of produce from the tomb of Kha at Deir el-Medîna was a pot containing some fatty matter, which was sent for analysis to a laboratory in Genoa. The fatty matter was determined as a mixture of various vegetable oils. Further analysis proved the presence of iron, which may have been due to the nature of the vessel in which the produce was prepared, or more

A woman pulling a rope(?) before a bouquet consisting of cornflowers, poppies and chrysanthemum(?). Relief from the temple of the Aten at el-Amarna; 18th Dynasty. Collection of E. Kofler, Lucerne.

likely, as the actual vessel in which it was found was of stone, the iron was added deliberately. A small proportion of resin was also detected in the substance. An experiment was carried out to determine whether other matters had been added. About 2cg of the substance was introduced subcutaneously into a frog. After half an hour the frog showed considerable excitement, leapt about, and reacted instantly to stimulus. After about one hour it calmed down and reacted very slowly. A larger quantity injected into another frog caused paralysis and death after the initial excitement. The drug was subsequently isolated, dissolved in water and injected into a frog and a mouse, causing heavy sleep, after which the two creatures returned to normal. The drug contained in the ancient substance was identified as morphine. Its ancient use remains obscure, but it is remarkable that after more than three thousand years the drug was still potent.

Peucedanum galbaniflora   Sulphur wort
Peucedanum officinale

Ancient Egyptian ?

Coptic: resin ⲭⲁⲗⲃⲁⲛⲏ

Greek: plant πευκέδανον; resin χαλβάνη

Modern Egyptian Arabic قنة *qina*

Peucedanum is an umbelliferous plant native to Persia, *P. galbaniflora* and *P. officinale* probably being known in antiquity. It produces a fragrant gum resin of a greenish tint known as *galbanum*, which was an ingredient in the famous Mendesian unguent (Pliny, *NH*.XIII.ii; Dioscorides 1.71; see above under 'Perfume'). In the Bible it is mentioned (called *ḥelbenah*) as being used for incense (Exodus 30:34). The 'green incense' mentioned in Egyptian texts may have been galbanum imported from Persia.

Theophrastus mentions that the plant grew in Arcadia, and that the root had warming properties used in a heating ointment, and it was also given in treatment of the spleen. But the seed and juice were useless, he claims (IX.20.2).

In Coptic medicine galbanum was used with other ingredients in a poultice for a wound and aching feet (Ch 15 and 13), and it was found useful to expel bugs from the home:

For all bugs when you wish to expel them from the house: a little galbanum, a little realgar, a little goat's fat. Place on the fire. [Add] bay berries. Steep it in water until it dissolves, and sprinkle the house with it. (WM7)

It should be mentioned that some scholars have suggested *Ferula galbaniflua* Boiss. as the source of galbanum.

Ancient Egyptian 𓃀𓈖𓂋𓏏 *bnrit*

Coptic: tree and fruit ⲃⲛⲛⲉ

Greek φοῖνιξ

Modern Egyptian Arabic: tree نخل *naḫl*; fruit بلح *balaḥ*

The date-palm has grown in Egypt since prehistoric times, and it is still a predominant feature of the landscape in the Nile Valley and the oases. The fruits are eaten fresh or dried, or they are distilled for various aperitifs and liqueurs. In some places a liquid is extracted from the trunk of the tree by affixing a vessel to the bleeding wound, an operation which eventually causes the tree to die. The

(*Right*) Girl with clusters of dates.
Wall-painting in Theban Tomb no. 38,
after a drawing by Hay; 18th Dynasty.
British Library (Hay MSS 29851, 294).

(*Below*) Date-palm. Wall-painting in
Theban Tomb no. 1; 19th Dynasty.

liquid is left to ferment and is enjoyed as an alcoholic beverage. This appears also to have been practised in ancient Assyria (the Assyrian Herbal § 37 A).

The inside of the very top of the palm trunk is edible, the taste being reminiscent of celery. This was used as part of the soldiers' diet in ancient Greece (Xenophon, *Anabasis* ii,iii), and the custom survives in modern Iraq.

In classical and pharaonic times wine was made from dates, and along with honey the juice of the fruit was one of the major sweetening agents in the days before sugar beet and sugar cane. The wine was drunk, but also used during the process of mummification to wash the body of the mummy. It was produced by steeping the dates in water and pressing out the liquid, which was then left to ferment. Dates appear to have been used for sweetening beer.

The fruits were pressed to blocks for easier handling, just as they are today, or they were threaded onto strings. They formed part of the wages paid to the workmen at Deir el-Medîna, along with bread, beer and vegetables. The wood of the trunk was used for roofing; the fibres for basketry; and the leaves for brushes and ropes. In medicine the dates or their juice were used for potions, suppositories, unguents and poultices:

A remedy for swelling of any limb of a man: fresh dates 1; date kernels 1; dry myrrh 1; wax 1; combine to a paste and bandage for four days. (H 235)

A remedy made for swollen and aching legs: red natron 1; is mixed with fermented date juice and the legs are bandaged therewith. (E 561)

A remedy to quell cough in a child: dried, crushed dates are ground in a *hin* of milk and drunk by the child. (Bln 30)

A remedy to kill worms: date kernels 1/8; carob pod pulp(?) 1/8; sweet beer 25 ro; is boiled, strained and drunk. Instant effect. (E 55)

A remedy to cure heat(?) of the heart: fresh dates 5 ro; honey 1/4; sweet beet 10 ro; administer to the anus for four days. (B 20)

A remedy for sneezing: date juice; fill the opening of the nose with it. (E 761)

A remedy to make the hair grow, made for Shesh, mother of his Majesty the King of Upper and Lower Egypt, Teti, justified: bone of a dog 1; date kernels 1; donkey's hoof 1; boil well in a jar with oil or fat and use as an unguent. (E 468)

Dates occur sparsely in Coptic remedies, once in a poultice with other ingredients for stomach ache (Ch 73). It is interesting that in traditional Islamic medicine dates were used for treating heart conditions, stomach-ache and as a prophylactic for poison and magic. Prospero Alpini quotes the Egyptians of his days as using date syrup with pomegranate as a laxative and to treat blood spitting (*Médicine*, 269). The Assyrian Herbal recommended date kernels ground in pork fat for swellings (§ 37 B).

Pimpinella anisum L.   Aniseed

Ancient Egyptian 𓇋𓈖𓋴𓏏 *inst*(?)

Coptic ?

Greek ἄνησσον

Modern Egyptian Arabic يانسون *jansôn*

Aniseed may be indigenous to Egypt and Asia Minor. It is now also cultivated in southern Europe. The fruits of the umbelliferous plant yield an essential oil, which in modern commercial products is frequently replaced by oil of Chinese star aniseed. The seeds have a strong aromatic flavour reminiscent of liquorice and very similar to fennel. They are carminative and digestive, soothe coughs and headaches and relieve catarrh. They also stimulate milk production. As an antiseptic they are sometimes used in toothpaste and to flavour toothpicks. Rubbed on cheese they are reputed to be an excellent bait for a mouse trap. Aniseed lends its characteristic aroma to aperitifs like Pernod, Ricard and Ouzo, Anisette being flavoured with star aniseed.

If the hieroglyphic name *inst* equals the almost synonymous aniseed, we can trace it in the pharaonic medical texts. It is employed internally for various stomach ailments and is chewed for toothache. One of the prescriptions suggests a refreshing drink:

A remedy, a fast acting drink to refresh the heart: figs 1/8; *inst* 1/8; ochre 1/8; honey 1/32; water 10 ro; is boiled and taken for four days. (E 235)

Another prescription concerns a cure for a bladder ailment:

A remedy for someone who suffers from contraction in the bladder: ox liver 1; *inst* 1; is baked and eaten by the patient. (E 267)

As aniseed is weakly diuretic, the remedy may have proved effective. An unspecified illness in the left part of the belly was treated with the following maceration:

figs 1/8; persea fruit (?) 1/64; grapes 2½ ro; *inst* 2½ ro; carob pod pulp(?) 1/8; gum 1/32; ochre 1/32; water 20 ro; is exposed to the dew overnight and drunk for four days. (E 633)

The Egyptian aniseed was said by Dioscorides to be second only to the Cretan sort, and he mentions its use in medicine (III.65). Apicius includes the herb in recipes of pork tripe, and he refers to a special kind of 'sweet wine biscuits' of which a recipe can be found in the writings of Cato (*De agricultura*, 121): 'Moisten 1 peck of wheat flour with must. Add aniseed, cumin, 2 lb fat, 1 lb cheese, and some grated bark of bay twig; shape and place each cake on a bay-leaf; then bake.' This recipe has been tried out by the translators of Apicius. They recommend 2oz of fat and 1oz of cheese to 2lb flour. Apicius served the cakes with cured pork.

Ancient Egyptian ?

Coptic ⲡⲓⲡⲉⲣ

Greek πέπερι

Modern Egyptian Arabic فلفل *felfel*

Pepper is a perennial shrub growing wild and now cultivated commercially in a number of countries. The leaves are glossy and ovate, the flower white, followed by round yellow to red fruit. It contains volatile oil and other constituents rendering it stomachic, carminative, antibacterial, insecticide, diaphoretic and, of course, stimulant and much favoured as a condiment. In East Africa it is used to induce abortion and as a mosquito repellant.

Prospero Alpini mentions pepper as an ingredient in recipes among others for sauces for grilled fish (x.1.6–8), and it is mentioned by Dioscorides (ii.189). The Copts used black as well as white pepper. The latter is used for:

someone with an aching anus: Knead with honey burnt wolf's dung ground with white pepper. Let the patient drink it. But first claim your fee. A proven remedy. (Ch 226)

The existence of pepper in ancient Egypt has recently been demonstrated by scientists examining the mummy of Ramesses ii. It appears that one of the ingredients used in the mummification of his body was black pepper. Pepper-corns were found lodged in his nostrils and abdomen.

Pisum sativum L.   Pea

Ancient Egyptian 𓏤𓇋𓏲𓆱𓏥 *thw*

Coptic ⲃⲉⲧⲃⲉⲧ

Greek πισός

Modern Egyptian Arabic بسلة *bisilla*

Peas were cultivated for human consumption. In Egypt they have been found in tombs from the Middle Kingdom onwards, but on sites in Anatolia and Greece dating to the sixth millennium BC and earlier remains prove their use even earlier.

In pharaonic medicine peas were included in mixtures to be taken, as well as for external application:

A remedy to open anything which has come by itself [that is a tumour or the like]: peas; Lower Egyptian salt; honey; combine and use as a bandage. (H 132)

A remedy to treat a humid spot at the toe nails: peas; carob pods(?); is pounded with honey and used as a bandage. (H 199)

A bandage consisting of peas and chopped leek was used to bandage a burn in order to 'make it black' and remove the white spots, after the wound had first been treated with red ochre pounded in sycamore juice and carob(?) (E 501).

Peas were mixed with acacia leaves, moringa oil, dry(?) oil, honey and an unidentified plant, and administered vaginally to stop a woman from bleeding (E 829). Stomach ailments were treated with a soothing beverage consisting of peas mixed with beer (E 4). Suffering inflicted by a demon or another mysterious source was conquered with beer mixed with coriander, peas and an unidentified ingredient to be taken before sleep (H 87).

Portulaca oleracea L.   Purslane

Ancient Egyptian 𓄇𓈖𓐍𓄇𓈖𓐍𓅓 *mḫmḫ*

Coptic ⲘⲈϨⲘⲞⲨϨⲈ

Greek ἀνδράχνη

Modern Egyptian Arabic رجلة *rigla*

Purslane grows wild in India and has been cultivated in Europe. It is an annual with succulent, edible stems, blunt leaves and yellow flowers. It is rich in vitamin C and has been used to treat scurvy. The leaves have a sharp flavour and can be used in salads when young, in stews when older. They can be applied to feverish brows with cooling effect and to inflamed eyes. The herb is diuretic. Prospero Alpini says that the poor in Egypt ate it mixed in yoghurt (*Médicine*, 252), and it was part of cooling beverages and enemas for patients with a temperature (*Médicine*, 266, 313).

Although purslane is conspicuously absent from medical texts, it occurs in other contexts which prove its presence in ancient Egypt. In Coptic medicine it is prescribed, as in more recent days, for inflamed eyes and skin diseases, and, internally, as a worm expellant:

An eye ointment for eyes suffering from rheuma. They will get well instantly: take purslane stems and grind them well and squeeze out the juices. Leave it in the shade with a little gum, make it into an ointment, and apply. (Ch 220)

Take fat and purslane juice. Make it into an ointment. Apply to the eye and it will heal. (Ch 96)

Burning, aching blisters in the skin: take leaves of willow, purslane, juice of nightshade, saffron, eggwhite, a little opium. Grind it with a little unmixed wine and apply. (Ch 215)

For inflamed breasts: take purslane, an egg and oil. Grind it together and apply to the breasts. They will be cured. (BA 8)

Another: purslane and goose fat. Grind it, and use as an unguent. (BKU 9)

A remedy for anything swollen: grind purslane and pork fat and apply. (BKU 3)

A remedy for someone who has worms in his stomach: take purslane, cow's milk, honey. Give the patient a mug full every day for three days. Boil it first. (Ch 110)

Potamogeton Schweinfurthii A. Benn.   Pondweed
syn. *P. lucens*

Ancient Egyptian ?

Coptic ?

Greek ποταμογείτων

Modern Egyptian Arabic حمول *ḥamûl* or جار النهر *gâr en-nahr* ('river neighbour')

Pondweed is an aquatic plant, almost totally submerged in water, the upper leaves sometimes floating on the surface. It grows in the Delta and in the Ismailiya Canal. In ancient Egypt it appears to have grown in Upper Egypt as well. It is represented on reliefs dating back to the Old Kingdom.

The ancient name for the plant was thought to be 𓈖𓈙𓄿𓅱 *nš3w*, but this has recently been demonstrated to be unlikely; *nš3w* occurs in the medical texts in poultices for stiff or broken limbs and as a vermifuge. In modern Egypt the fruits are used for their astringent and refreshing effect.

Prunus dulcis (Mill.) D. A. Webb   Almond
syn. *P. amygdalus* Batsch

Ancient Egyptian ˁwnt(?)

Coptic ?

Greek ἀμυγδαλῆ

Modern Egyptian Arabic: nuts لوز *lôz*

The almond tree is native to central Asia. It is rare in Egypt nowadays, as it appears to have been in ancient times as well. The almonds were imported, presumably from Greece. Some were found in the tomb of Tutankhamun in a jar labelled ˁwnt.

The nuts were presumably eaten, and almond oil was used for unguents. It is emollient, demulcent and laxative. Essential oil of bitter almonds is poisonous, containing prussic acid. Prospero Alpini tells that Egyptian women consumed sweet almonds to gain weight (*Médicine*, 233–4), and that the nuts were used to clarify Nile water (*Médicine*, 36). Bitter almond oil was used in massage to bring about perspiration (*Médicine*, 318, 321).

Punica granatum L.   Pomegranate

Ancient Egyptian 𓇋𓈖𓎛𓏠𓈖 *inhmn*

Coptic ⲉⲣⲙⲁⲛ

Greek: tree ῥόα; flower κύτινος; rind σίσιον

Modern Egyptian Arabic رمان *rummân*

The pomegranate grows wild in south-west Asia and is cultivated in Mediterranean countries. It is a shrub or tree with scarlet, scented flowers and later a hard yellowish fruit full of bright-red seeds. The tree was introduced into Egypt in the New Kingdom. It was one of the trees planted in the garden of Ineni at Thebes (see above, under 'The Egyptian Garden'), and Tuthmosis III brought it back from exploits into Asia and depicted it in his 'botanical garden'.

A flowering pomegranate tree.
Wall-painting in Theban Tomb no. 217;
Ramesside.

In the Graeco-Roman world the pomegranate was synonymous with fertility. The inside of the fruit yields the true grenadine, and the fresh juice is a favourite drink in Cairo. The bark of the trunk and the root are used in medicine, as they contain tannin, particularly efficient for expelling tapeworm, a fact already discovered by the ancient Egyptians. The classical authors mention wine made from pomegranate juice, which was according to Dioscorides used for medicinal purposes (v.34). Prospero Alpini says that one of the treatments for plague fever consisted of a certain beverage to which was added wine made from sour pomegranates (*Médicine*, 320).

In ancient Egypt the fruit was consumed, and the flowers set in bouquets and garlands. The rind was used to dye leather yellow (Pliny, *NH*.XIII.xxxiv). In modern Iraq it is used for similar purposes, mixed with water. The fruit and its rounded shape caused a comparison to be made between a woman's breast and the yellow fruit, and her teeth were compared to its glistening seeds.

Pomegranate may be used in the treatment of dysentery, diarrhoea and stomach-ache. In Egypt it was used for similar complaints:

To kill roundworm: root of pomegranate 5 ro; water 10 ro; remains in the dew overnight and is taken for one day. (E 50)

Another excellent remedy for the belly: root of pomegranate is pounded with beer 5 ro, and is left in a jar with water 15 ro overnight. Strain in a cloth, and give it to the patient to drink. (E 63)

If *nurmû* in the Assyrian Herbal is pomegranate, its juice was here prescribed to treat eyes and ears; as an enema; in massage with fish oil; and in poultices for burns and swelling. The rind was used 'to bind the stomach' (§ 39), a practice also recorded by Dioscorides (I.153). The use of pomegranate as a laxative appears to have been carried on by the Copts, and the rind boiled with water was used to treat a skin ailment (ZB 21). For a remedy to treat blood in the mouth, see

A bowl of pomegranates.
British Museum.

Carrying provisions to the tomb: a large bunch of onions, and baskets of loaves(?) and pomegranates. Wall-painting in Theban Tomb no. 113 (now destroyed), after a drawing by Hay; Ramesside. British Library (Hay MSS 29822, 124).

above under *Foeniculum vulgare*. Prospero Alpini gives a recipe for a mildly laxative syrup consisting of 2½ parts juice of unripe dates, 1 part sour pomegranates and 5 parts sugar (*Médicine*, 269, cf. 10).

Raphanus sativus L. Radish

Ancient Egyptian 𓂝𓈖𓏥 *smw*(?) and/or 𓈖𓏌𓈖 *nwn*(?)

Coptic ⲤⲒⲘ

Greek ῥαφανίς

Modern Egyptian Arabic فجل *figl*

A 20–30cm-tall plant with lilac flowers and a bulbous root, which is the part used for culinary purposes. Its juice has been known to treat gallstone, kidney complaints and breathing disorders. It is laxative, slightly narcotic and stimulates the appetite, and it may be used for headaches and rheumatism.

Radishes were known to the classical authors, including Pliny, who comments on Egyptian radishes saying that in that country radishes were a most profitable crop, and that the roots were remarkably sweet. He also quotes the Egyptians for using it for medicinal purposes (*NH*.XIX.xxvi–lxxxvi). Dioscorides says that some use radish oil to treat skin diseases, but the Egyptians for cooking (1.45). The Copts used radish seeds to treat internal complaints (Ryl 4) and its oil for cooking and anointing. The Assyrian Herbal identifies radish as PUGLU (cf. Arabic *figl*). But perhaps the most notorious reference to radishes stems from some translations of Herodotus (II.125) quoting him as saying that the pyramid-builders received their pay in 'radishes, onions and garlic'. The word for 'radish' (συϱμαία) is somewhat disputed since it actually denotes a laxative (which could of course have been prepared from radishes). This 'syrmaia' was also used as a cheap substance in mummification (II.88), for which the use of radishes has not been proven, although radishes have been found in excavations of material dating to the Middle Kingdom.

Ricinus communis L.   Castor-oil plant

Ancient Egyptian ⌐⧖🐦⧗ *dgm*
Coptic: plant ⲦⲎϬⲘⲈϬ; seeds ⲔⲓⲔⲓ
Greek: plant ϰϱότων; seeds ϰίϰι
Modern Egyptian Arabic خروع *ḥarwa*

A perennial plant with palmate leaves which may grow as tall as a tree. The seed capsules are bur-like, the oval glossy seeds black, red, white or mottled with an agreeable nutty taste. The plant is indigenous to Africa. It still grows wild, but is extensively cultivated for industrial purposes. It has been used in folk medicine from most ancient times, especially its leaves and seeds. However, it is a dangerous plant containing poisonous ricin. A few seeds are known to have been fatal even to adults, and cattle and poultry have been poisoned. In parts of Africa mixing castor seeds with food is a well-known means of infanticide, and the oil is used to poison cockroaches. Minute amounts of castor bean allergen may cause acute respiratory reactions. In Egypt the plant is sown around houses to repel mosquitoes. In spite of its toxicity, the young fruits and the oil are consumed and added to commercially produced goods.

Seeds of the castor-oil plant have been found in prehistoric burials in Egypt, and there is ample evidence of their use. Among the classical authors, Herodotus (II.94), Diodorus (I.34), Strabo (XVII.2.5) and Pliny (*NH*.xv.vii) mention the use of castor oil in Egypt as a lamp oil. Strabo adds that the poorer people used the oil for anointing the body. The oil was extracted, they say, either by bruising and pressing the seeds, or by roasting and boiling them and skimming the oil, or by grinding the seeds in a mill, putting the mass into baskets and pressing out the oil (Dioscorides I.38). Another technique was to sprinkle the seeds with oil and press them.

One of the medical texts includes a short essay entirely devoted to the use of the castor oil plant:

Knowing what can be made from the castor oil plant, something found in ancient writings, something useful to man.

Crush the root in water. Place it on the head which suffers. The patient will soon feel as well as one who is not ill.

Chew a little of the fruit with beer if the patient has *why* in his faeces. This is to cure illness of the belly of the patient. The fruit will cause the hair of a woman to grow. Pound it, make it into a paste, steep it in oil. The woman shall rub her head with it.

Oil can be made out of the fruit to anoint a patient who suffers from a skin disease. He will be like someone to whom nothing has happened. He shall be anointed for ten days, early, so that the disease goes away. Really efficient, tried a million times. (E 251)

Castor oil is indeed both purgative and emollient. It was, incidentally, one of the commodities which the workmen at Deir el-Medîna received at regular intervals. It was especially intended for anointing, and it cost half the price of sesame oil, which was in turn used for human consumption.

Castor-oil 'fruits' are specified in a number of pharaonic prescriptions:

To expel illness in all limbs of a patient: fruit of the castor oil plant is pounded and mixed with honey and [the limb] is bandaged with it. (E 601)

A remedy to treat *hnsyt*-illness in the head: fruit of the castor-oil plant 1; ox fat 1; moringa oil; is combined to a paste and used as an unguent every day. (E 437)

A remedy to empty the bowels and to treat pain in the belly of the patient: fruit of the castor-oil plant are chewed and swallowed with beer so that whatever is in his belly comes out. (E 25)

The leaf of the plant was used as a bandage to hold in place a vegetable paste applied to a burn, accompanied by a recitation of a magical formula (L 46). Along with other herbs, the fruits were burnt as fumigation to expel a disease caused by a demon (Bln 58).

The use of castor beans was continued by the Copts, and they are prescribed in a few texts:

A remedy for the glands: castor-oil seeds; tragant gum; salt; wild chicory. Pound it and apply it as a powder. (Ch 223)

An 'excellent remedy' for an unspecified disease consisted of resin, castor-oil seeds, wax and radish oil boiled together (Ch 117), and a healing poultice for a wound was mixed from:

capers 8 drachma; alum 4 drachma; aristolochia 4 drachma; castor-oil seeds 4 drachma. Pound it, boil it with honey. Apply it to the skin, and the wound will dry up. (Ch 135)

Rosmarinus officinalis L. Rosemary

Ancient Egyptian ?
Coptic ?
Greek λιβανωτίς
Modern Egyptian Arabic حصلبان *ḥaṣalbân*

Rosemary grows wild in European Mediterranean countries and is cultivated in Egyptian gardens. Whether it was grown in ancient times remains uncertain. Prospero Alpini had an opportunity to examine a mummy in Cairo and claims that he found branches of rosemary in the wrappings. As he had a sound knowledge of plants there is no reason to doubt his evidence. The ancient name of the plant being unknown, it is not possible to establish whether rosemary was used for any other purpose.

Today rosemary has a variety of uses as a carminative, digestive and antiseptic. Its oil is rubbed into tired limbs; rosemary tea is thought to cure headache; and it is frequently recommended in hair and skin care. The branches are used in fumigation, and sprigs of rosemary flavour stews, fish, puddings and ale.

Rubia tinctorum L. Madder

Ancient Egyptian 𓎛𓇥𓅓𓏺 *ip3*
Coptic ⲁⲡⲉⲓ
Greek ερυθράδανον
Modern Egyptian Arabic فوة *fôa*

Madder is a perennial plant with a long climbing and scabrous stem, the lanceolate leaves being arranged in whorls. It has pale-green flowers and red globular berries. The roots of the plant contain a red colouring matter which is used for dyeing. According to Dioscorides (III.60) the Egyptians called it *sophoboi*. It is mentioned by Pliny as a treatment for jaundice (*NH*.XXIV.xxvii).

In modern Egyptian folk medicine the powdered root is employed as a tonic, to ease childbirth and to treat bladder ailments. It is now imported from Asia Minor.

Ruta graveolens L.   Rue

Ancient Egyptian ?

Coptic: *R. sylvestris* ⲃⲁϣⲟⲩϣ

Greek πήγανον

Modern Egyptian Arabic فيجن *fîgan*; سداب *sadâb*

Rue is a semi-evergreen perennial growing to 1m. It has greyish-green oblong leaves and small yellow flowers. It contains volatile oil and many active substances, and is thus a most useful ingredient in herbal medicine. It is emmenagogue, antihelmitic, stomachich and diaphoretic. It has been used to treat epilepsy and, externally, for skin diseases, rheumatism and as an eye lotion and gargle. The leaves can be used in salads and the oil in perfume.

Prospero Alpini quotes the Egyptians of his day as using the oil for massage for feverish conditions 'like the ancients did it'. Alternatively, the back of the patient could be rubbed with equal quantities of mature oil, rue juice and aromatic white wine, with the addition of a composite remedy. The mixture was then boiled and reduced to half (*Médicine*, 318). The herb was known to Theophrastus and Dioscorides, and it seems to have been prescribed in the Assyrian Herbal as *anameru* (§ 10 U cf. *šibburatu*, § 108). The Copts knew rue and a 'wild rue', the latter having been identified as *Peganum harmala* L. They used rue mainly to treat skin diseases, but also for worms and sick testicles:

willow branches; fresh rue; grind it with wine. Give it to the sick man to drink and they will get well. (Ch 170)

'Wild rue', on the other hand, was applied to a tooth to facilitate extraction (Ch 184).

Salix suberrata Willd. syn. *Salix safsaf* Forrsk.   Willow

Ancient Egyptian ⲧⲣⲧ *trt*

Coptic ⲁⲥⲥⲁⲩⲥⲁⲩ; var. *Salix alba* ⲧⲱⲣⲉ

Greek ἰτεά

Modern Egyptian Arabic صفصاف *ṣafṣâf*

In recent times the discovery of the medicinal properties of willow bark revolutionised pharmacology. Salicyl is strongly antiseptic and was successfully used to treat rheumatism until a similar chemical agent took over. Although the ancient Egyptians used willow leaves and willow 'fruits', there is no indication that they had discovered the true value of the willow tree in medicine.

The willow tree had an ancient history there, the earliest finds dating from the very beginning of history. A few isolated objects of willow wood have been excavated, and willow leaves were found in the tomb of Tutankhamun. The tree grew in Egypt in the New Kingdom. There is a record of a weary traveller to the Valley of the Kings in Ramesside times who sat down in the shade of a willow tree in the otherwise barren rocky valley and spent his hour of leisure measuring out the distance between the tombs he could see from his resting place in the shade. Nowadays the willow tree still grows in Egypt, and its wood is used for making camel saddles, vine supports, and parts of the screw of Archimedes, the cylinder which, combined with human agency, transfers water from a canal to fields at a higher level.

The Egyptian physicians prescribed willow leaves and fruits for a number of ailments. The leaves were part of a remedy to stimulate the appetite; the fruits were used with other ingredients in a bandage for swelling and in an unguent for inflammation. Whatever antiseptic properties remained in the tiny willow twigs were badly needed here, for the remedy also contained hippopotamus dung. One remedy was used to dry out the ear:

acacia leaves; zizyphus leaves; willow fruit; cumin; is made into a powder and applied. (E 766c)

Another consisted of a cooling bandage to be laid on a limb when a broken bone had been set:

acacia leaves; willow leaves; sycamore leaves; emmer grains; gum water; bandage for four days. (H 234)

A pollarded willow. Wall-painting in Theban Tomb no. 217; Ramesside.

With other plants and a liquid it was used as a fumigation for toothache (Bln 75), and with acacia leaves, zizyphus leaves, salt, onions and another plant it was used as a bandage (H 95). An inflamed breast was treated with a bandage of willow and zizyphus leaves and another unidentified ingredient (Sm 41).

In Coptic medicine willow found use in a remedy for burning, aching blisters along with other herbs (see above under *Portulaca oleracea*, but this was probably the *Salix alba* variety) and in treatment for the testicles (see above under *Ruta graveolens*). Burnt willow leaves and rose oil were used to treat the skin disease called *psora* (Ch 231). The ashes of *S. safsaf* were used to treat another, unspecified illness (MK 2).

Sesamum indicum L.   Sesame

Ancient Egyptian: plant 𓇋𓆟𓏤 *ikw*; oil 𓈖� *nḥḥ*

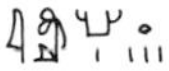

Coptic: plant ⲟⲕⲉ; seeds ⲥⲓⲙⲥⲓⲙ

Greek σήσαμον

Modern Egyptian Arabic سمسم *simsim*

Sesame is an annual plant growing to 90cm, with oblong leaves, purple or whitish flowers and a 3cm-long capsule containing flat seeds. It is native to tropical climates and is widely cultivated for its seeds, which yield the valuable sesame oil. It is nutritive, laxative and emollient. The leaves and seeds may be used as a poultice, and the ground seeds with water added may be used to treat haemorrhoids; the Indians use them as an emmenagogue. Apart from their multiple use in medicine, the seeds are sprinkled on bread or ground to a paste, *tahina*, a favoured condiment in Arab countries dating back to the time of Prospero Alpini, if not much earlier.

The ancient Egyptian word *šmšmt* was in the past wrongly taken to mean sesame, but has now been shown to be *Cannabis sativa*. In the Mesopotamian area there is a similar problem with a word being translated 'sesame' or 'flax'.

In ancient Egypt the oil was used for unguents and as a lamp oil, and for the workmen at Deir el-Medîna it was a major part of the diet. It does not occur in any of the standard medical texts, possibly because the plant was only introduced after the texts were compiled. Dioscorides knew that the Egyptians made sesame oil (II.121). The Copts used the leaves boiled with water as a poultice (ZB 30), and the boiled seeds were eaten by women to help lactation (BA 7), a custom still used in India. Remains of sesame were found in the tomb of Tutankhamun.

Sinapis alba L.   White mustard

Ancient Egyptian ? (Demotic *ḫltm*)

Coptic ϭⲓⲛⲁⲡⲉ or ϢⲀⲀⲦⲀⲘ

Greek σίναπη

Modern Egyptian Arabic حردل – *ḥardal*

Mustard is a branched annual growing to 1m; the stems are slightly hairy, the leaves oval and lobed. The flowers are yellow, and the seeds, set in pods, are yellowish. The plant is native to southern Europe and western Asia. It is cultivated commercially for culinary purposes. In medicine it is used as a stimulant, irritant and emetic. A variety of mustard was included in the Assyrian Herbal as HALDAPPÂNU. It was used to treat swelling, cough, jaundice and stomach ailments and toothache, and it was administered as an enema or used as a mouthwash.

Dioscorides uses the word λαμψάνη for mustard and says that the Egyptians called it *euthmoi* (II.142). The Copts used two words for mustard, one taken from the Greek, the other obviously from the Assyrian designation, which also appeared in the late form of Egyptian called Demotic. The Copts used mustard to treat headache:

For painful, aching temples: wheatmeal 2 drachma; mustard 1 drachme; a little vinegar. Grind well and apply. (Ch 160)

Internally it was used for flatulence:

cumin; pepper; rue; mustard; Arabic natron; honey. Grind well, give to the patient to eat and he will get well. (Ch 69)

Solanum dulcamara L.   Woody nightshade

Ancient Egyptian ?

Coptic ?

Greek: *S. nigrum* στρύχνος

Modern Egyptian Arabic حلوة مرة – *ḥelwa murra* ('bitter sweet')

A shrubby perennial growing to 2m or more, with ovate leaves, violet flowers and red berries. It is a poisonous plant, the medicinal qualities of which have been recognised since the Middle Ages. The raw berries are highly poisonous, but the substance partly breaks down in solution and is capable of affecting the nervous system. The poisonous stems are used to treat asthma, catarrh, rheumatism and bronchitis. In India it is considered diuretic and is used to treat syphilis.

The plant was known to the ancient Egyptians, as remains were found in the tomb of Tutankhamun, but its use remains conjectural. The variety *Solanum nigrum*, with white flowers and black berries, was known to the Copts as ⲈⲖⲟⲟⲗⲉ ⲚⲞⲨⲰⲚⲰ ('wolf grapes'). They used it in a soothing unguent including willow leaves, purslane, saffron, eggwhite and opium (Ch 215). In Arabic the berries are known as عنب التعلب *'inab-el-taʿlab* ('fox grapes'). Pliny mentions that the ancient Egyptian florists used 'trychnos' in their chaplets because of its similarity to ivy (*NH*.XXI.cv).

Tamarix nilotica Ehrenb. and *Tamarix articulata* Vahl Tamarisk

Ancient Egyptian 𓇔 *isr*

Coptic ⲞⲤⲒ

Greek: *T. articulata* μυρίκη

Modern Egyptian Arabic: *T. nilotica* أثل *atl*; *T. articulata* صرفاء *ṭarfa*; gall تمر الأثل *tamr el-atl*

A tamarisk tree(?).
Wall-painting in Theban
Tomb no. 49;
18th Dynasty.

Tamarisk shrubs or trees with their green or greyish foliage, growing on the edge of the desert, are indigenous to Egypt. The fruits are capsules with several seeds having tufts of hair at the top. The 'fruits' mentioned in the texts may refer to the pellets of gall deposited on the branches by insects, a commodity still for sale for tanning purposes.

Dioscorides says that the 'fruit' was used in an infusion for the eyes (I.118), and the 'fruit' was also referred to by Prospero Alpini (*Médicine*, 313, 314; *Plantes*, 33). The Assyrian Herbal prescribes tamarisk for a wide variety of ailments (§ 29B). In modern Egyptian folk medicine it is used to treat the eyes, haemorrhages and dysentery, and when ground it is used as a tooth powder.

The ancient Egyptians used the wood in carpentry, and the 'fruit' was used in medicine:

A remedy to expel an evil inflammation: alum 1; red ochre 1; 'fruit' of tamarisk 1; natron 1; salt 1; are mixed together and applied. (E 96)

A bandage of tamarisk twigs and an unidentified plant was applied to 'soothe the vessels' (H 102). Prospero Alpini quotes the use of a decoction of the wood to treat leprosy and ulcers (*Plantes*, 33), and a decoction of the bark administered to the vagina to stop menstruation (*ibid.*).

Thymus syn. *Thymbra* (species unknown)   Thyme

Ancient Egyptian 𓃂𓏏𓇋𓏏𓏥 *t3iti* (?)

Coptic ⲔⲢⲒⲘⲂⲞⲚ

Greek: *T. capitata*, Cretan thyme θύμος

Modern Egyptian Arabic زعتر *zaʿtar*

Although the ancient name for thyme has not yet been proven with absolute certainty, there is evidence of the plant having been known, if not grown, in Egypt. Dioscorides says that the Egyptians called a variety of the plant *merouopyos* (III.46). This has been identified as *T. sibthorpii*, the Greek ἕρπυλος. Remains of *T. spicata*, according to Dioscorides called *saem* by the Egyptians (III.30) were found in the tomb of Tutankhamun.

Thyme grows in Egypt today, and Apicius used the herb in several recipes. It is an important flavouring in Mediterranean cooking, and thyme honey from the slopes of Hymettos hills in Greece is justly famous. The leaves contain the antiseptic thymol which is widely used in modern pharmacy as an antispasmodic, antiseptic, expectorant and carminative. Pliny refers to two kinds of thyme used to treat headaches and intestinal complaints (*T. vulgaris* and *T. serpyllum*?) (*NH*.XX, xc). The Assyrian Herbal quotes thyme (*hašu*) in treatment of lung and stomach ailments (§ 59).

Ancient Egyptian 𓏏𓏤𓄿𓍿𓄿𓏏 *ḥm3yt* (?)

Coptic ⲦⲒⲀⲒ

Greek βουϰέϱας or τῆλις

Modern Egyptian Arabic حلبة *ḥilba*

Fenugreek is an annual herb with trifoliate leaves and whitish flowers followed by a beaked pod which contains 10 to 20 seeds. It appears to be indigenous to the Mediterranean, and remains have been found from as early as 3000 BC. The plant is a member of the pea family. The pods contain seeds of a yellowish-brown colour, almost odourless unless subjected to heat. They are rich in vitamins, nitrates and calcium, properties which may have influenced a prescription for rejuvenation of pharaonic date which has as its sole ingredient a plant named *ḥm3yt*, very likely our fenugreek (although 'bitter almond' has also been suggested). The seeds are thought to encourage lactation and heal inflammations. They are a frequent ingredient in curry spice, and are in Egypt added to bread. The leaves are used as a vegetable, and also as fodder. The sprouted seed is a palatable salad herb.

Among the classical authors Theophrastus mentions fenugreek, calling it an Indian plant (IV.4.10). Dioscorides says that the Egyptians called it *itasin* (II.124). Fenugreek seeds were found in the tomb of Tutankhamun. In ancient Egypt the herb was used to induce childbirth:

A remedy to loosen a child in the womb of a woman: fresh *ḥm3yt* 1; honey 1; is strained and taken for one day. (E 801)

Another remedy for the same purpose was a vaginal suppository made of incense, onions, beer, fresh *ḥm3yt*, fly dung and an unidentified plant (E 802). Dioscorides also prescribes a decoction of the seeds to treat the vulva (I.124). Furthermore, fenugreek was made into an ointment which must have been much in demand:

The beginning of the book of making an old man into a young man. You must collect a great quantity of *ḥm3yt*, about two sacks full. Then you shall break them up and leave them in the sun. When they are completely dry, you shall thresh them like you would thresh barley. Then you must winnow it down to the last pod. All that has come out of it must be measured and sifted. Divide it into two portions, one consisting of the seeds, the other of the pods, of equal quantity. Then you shall place them in water, the two portions having been combined. Knead it to a dough. Place it in a new [clean] pot on the fire and boil it for a long time. You will recognise when it is done when the water has evaporated and they dry up until they are as dry as straw with no moisture at all. Take them away from the fire.

When they have cooled, place them in a pot and wash them in the river. Wash them thoroughly. You will know when they are washed enough when you taste the water in the pot and there is no bitter taste left. Then you shall leave them in the sun spread out on a piece of laundryman's cloth. When they are dry, you shall grind them on the mill stone until they have been reduced to small pieces.

Then you shall steep them in water and make them into a soft dough. Then you shall place them in a vessel on the fire and cook them for a long time. You will know when they are done when the pellets of oil rise to the surface. All the time you must skim the oil which has risen with a spoon. Place it in the jar whose inner surface has been plastered with clay, smooth and thick. Skim the oil and strain it into the jar through a cloth. Then you shall place it in a jar of stone and use it as an unguent. It is a remedy for illness in the head. When the body is rubbed with it, the skin is left beautiful without any blemishes. It is a million times efficient. (Sm 21, 9–22, 10)

The use of clay mentioned above was either to make the jar extra watertight, or perhaps it added smoothness to the remedy: Pliny tells that the Greeks 'enlivened the smoothness of their wines with potter's earth' (*NH*.XIV.xxiv).

Prospero Alpini mentions fenugreek as an ingredient in a pain-killing mixture and a poultice to treat fever (*Médicine*, 266, 318). It was considered a 'warming' herb (*Médicine*, 253) and poor people used it to gain weight (*Médicine*, 236).

Triticum dicoccum Schrank.   Emmer

Ancient Egyptian 𓆷𓏏𓏏 *bdt*

Coptic ⲃⲱⲧⲉ

Greek ζεια

Modern Egyptian Arabic ?

Emmer was grown in Egypt from the earliest times. It was widely used for making bread and beer. Flour made from emmer is 'weak', suitable for flat breads and pastry. It was the staple crop in ancient Mesopotamia until it was replaced by barley.

In medicine, emmer was used in bandages. With salt and another plant it was believed to induce childbirth (E 800). It was employed to stimulate the growth of hair, although it is not quite clear which part of the plant was used, since it contained a certain amount of liquid. The relevant part of the plant was ground in a mortar, squeezed through cloth and the resulting liquid mixed to a paste with honey and oil and boiled, then applied to the bald patch (H 145). There is also a recipe for refreshing 'emmer water':

A remedy to treat the heart: black emmer 20 ro; water 160 ro; is boiled, strained, reduced to 35 ro and drunk for four days. (H 51)

Along with barley, emmer was used in birth prognoses (see above under *Hordeum vulgare*). The grains of emmer were also known as 𓃭𓃭 *mimi*. They were used to treat a cough:

emmer grain flour 5 ro; goose fat 5 ro; honey 5 ro; is boiled and eaten for four days (E 318)

Another remedy for cough in the belly: dried grains of emmer are mixed with beer and placed in a hot vessel and made to a sheet. Is eaten for four days. (E 322)

The result was probably a kind of beer biscuit baked on the inside of the pot.

Emmer grains mixed with water(?) and strained were thought to ease constipation (E 203). A similar mixture, exposed to the dew overnight, was used as a compress for the eyes (Ram III A 25–6). A poultice for swollen legs consisted of emmer grains, honey and wine (Bln 125).

Emmer grains were part of a treatment to prevent a woman from conceiving. The physician would first perform a fumigation with emmer grains at the genitalia of the woman, apparently with the purpose of preventing penetration. The treatment was concluded by drinking a concoction of oil 5 ro, celery 5 ro and sweet beer 5 ro for four consecutive mornings (Bln 192).

Vicia ervilia (L.) Willd. — Bitter vetch

Ancient Egyptian ?

Coptic ⲞⲨⲢⲞⲂⲞⲨ

Greek ὄροβος

Modern Egyptian Arabic كرسنة *kirsanna*

Bitter vetch is a pulse at present grown only for fodder in the Middle East. The seeds are toxic. They have been found in Mesopotamia (*c.* 2000 BC), and the plant was known in the Assyrian Herbal (*kiššenu* cf. p. 278). Finds in Anatolia go back as far as 5600 BC. The plant was discussed in detail by Theophrastus, and the Copts used vetch flour in composite remedies, among other things in external remedies to treat teeth and gums:

incense 2 drachma; starch 2 drachma; vetch. Grind and apply. (Ch 180)

Seeds of *Vicia sativa* have been found in an Egyptian burial of the Old Kingdom, which suggests that the plant was also known to the ancient Egyptians.

Vicia faba L. — Broad bean

Ancient Egyptian 𓊪𓅱𓂋 *pwr*

Coptic ⲫⲉⲗ

Greek κύαμος

Modern Egyptian Arabic فول *fōl*

The bean is an erect annual growing to a height of 1m. White flowers turn to pods with 3 to 6 seeds. A smaller bean, *V. faba equina* Pers. ('horse bean') has been found in Iraq (*c.*2300 BC), and in Jerico as early as 6000 BC.

Boiled broad beans are the national dish of Egypt, loved by rich and poor alike. 'Beans have satisfied even the pharaohs' is an Arab saying. This is undoubtedly true, for beans have been found in burials dating back to the 5th Dynasty.

Vigna sinensis (L.) Endl.   Bean
(= *Dolichos lubia* Forssk.)

Ancient Egyptian   𓇌𓏤𓏤𓏥 *iwryt*

Coptic ογρω

Greek ἄραχος or φάσηλος

Modern Egyptian Arabic لوبيا *lubyâ* or لبلاب *lablâb*

Beans have been found in Egypt from the Old Kingdom onwards. In spite of the fact that certain taboos were concerned with the consumption of beans, they were nevertheless eaten. The workmen at Deir el-Medîna received beans as part of their wages. Herodotus claims that the Egyptians did not even grow beans, and those that might grow were left alone. The priests were not even supposed to look at them, as they were considered impure (II.37). In modern Egyptian folk medicine they are prescribed as an aphrodisiac. In pharaonic medicine bean meal was used to treat constipation:

Bean meal 2½ ro, sifted through a cloth; water 20 ro, boiled; is given as an enema with instant effect. (Bln 164c)

Another enema: bean meal 1/32; salt 1/32; oil or fat 2½ ro; honey 1/4; sweet beer 25 ro; is administered to the anus for four days. (B 28)

A masticatory for a sick tongue was mixed from acacia leaves, ochre, beans, Nubian haematite, calcite powder, honey, another plant and an unidentified ingredient (E 704). An unguent to treat a urinary complaint in a male patient consisted of:

stem of rush 1; boiled beans 1; is mixed with oil or fat and the member anointed therewith. (E 270)

Beans frequently occur in unguents or bandages to treat the 'vessels'. Other varieties of the bean were employed in Coptic medicine.

Vitex agnus-castus L.   Chaste tree

Ancient Egyptian 𓊪𓂝𓈖𓃀𓏤𓏥 *s῾3m* (?)

Coptic ϣⲎⲦⲤ

Greek ἄγνος (= οῖσος)

Modern Egyptian Arabic: plant بنجنكشت *bengenkušt* or كيف ماريام *kêf mâryâm* ('Maria's pleasure'); seeds حب الفقد *ḥabb el-faqad*

Chaste tree is an aromatic shrub, native to southern Europe. It has palmate leaves and lavender-coloured flowers. The seeds contain a hormone-like substance which is now used in gynaecological medicine to treat premenstrual tension. It reduces libido in the male (hence the modern name of the shrub). These qualities do not appear to have been recognised by the Egyptians.

The chaste tree has been tentatively identified with *s῾3m* of the Egyptian texts (Dioscorides I.135: *sum*). It occurs in prescriptions for bandages. With ground barley, red ochre and an unidentified ingredient it was thought to ease swelling (E 590). Ground *s῾3m* mixed with water was used to strengthen the teeth (E 744). With other ingredients it was prescribed for constipation (E 23). In the Assyrian Herbal it has been identified as *šunû*. A diuretic and emmenagogue, it was prescribed for a number of ailments (§ 35).

Vitis vinifera L.   Vine

Ancient Egyptian: grapes 𓇋𓃀𓂋𓂋𓏏 *i3rrt*; raisins �wnši *wnši*

Coptic: plant and grapes ⲈⲖⲟⲟⲖⲈ; raisins ⲈⲖⲈⲬϢⲞⲨϢⲞⲨ

Greek: plant ἄμπελος; grapes σταφυλή

Modern Egyptian Arabic: plant and grapes عنب *'inab*; raisins زبيب *zibîb*

A vigorous vine. Relief from the temple of Aten at el-Amarna; 18th Dynasty. Schimmel collection, New York.

Grapes can be grown in Egypt wherever the soil and water conditions are favourable, thus almost anywhere. Least suited are the regions of Qena and Aswân in Upper Egypt because of the excessive heat; nevertheless, vines are planted there. In pharaonic Egypt the best vineyards were in the Delta and in the oases, but even in Nubia and the Sudan attempts were made to grow vines.

The grapes are eaten and are used for making wine, and the leaves are wrapped round rice or meat and eaten. In pharaonic medicine wine was a common vehicle for other ingredients; the dregs were sometimes used as well. A laxative consisted of:

wine 1; honey 1; cyperus rhizomes ['tiger nuts'] 1; is strained and drunk for one day. (E 12)

A chest remedy included:

carob pod pulp(?) 1/16; cumin 1/4; wine. Is boiled and drunk for four days. (E 183)

A drink to stimulate the appetite was made from:

wine 2½ ro; wheat gruel 1/8; is left in the dew overnight, strained and drunk for one day. (E 287)

Wine with frankincense and honey was believed to kill worm (Bln 7); with dill it eased pain (H 44); and with salt it cured a cough (Bln 39). In all these instances the effect was due not so much to the wine as to the additional ingredients.

Raw grapes were an ingredient in a soothing drink to treat a demonic disease along with figs, notched sycamore figs and honey, all to be boiled in cow's milk (Bln 114). In other remedies grapes or raisins occur along with other fruits, particularly figs and *išd* (persea?).

In Coptic medicine the leaves were used to treat warts, ground with water and applied (WB 40). Grape juice was a vehicle for other ingredients in lotions for the breasts and the male member (BA 2). Prospero Alpini mentions the use of wine leaves in lukewarm baths to treat fever (*Médicine*, 246).

A bowl of raisins.
British Museum.

Ancient Egyptian 𓈖𓊪𓊃 *nbs*

Coptic: tree ΝΟΥΒⲤ; fruit ⲔⲈΝΝⲀⲢⲈ

Greek παλίουϱος ὁ Αἰγύπτιος

Modern Egyptian Arabic: tree سدر *sidr*; fruit نبق *nabq*

Zizyphus is a shrub or tree with glabrous branches. The wild variety has spikes below the greyish-green tough leaves. It has clustered yellowish flowers and berries that look like wild cherries. In its cultivated state it grows in Egyptian gardens today, and it still grows wild in Upper Egypt and Nubia. It is a popular fruit, and is also used in folk medicine. It was equally favoured in pharaonic times, and dried fruits have been found in predynastic graves. Some were included in the burial equipment of Tutankhamun.

The tree is frequently mentioned by the classical authors, and Theophrastus gives a description of the appearance of the Egyptian tree. It is 'more shrubby that the lotus [sc. *Zizyphus lotus*, a shrub which now grows around the Mediterranean]; it has a leaf like the tree of the same name in our country, but the fruit is different; for it is not flat, but round and red, and in size as large as the fruit of the prickly cedar or a little larger; it has a stone which is not eaten with the fruit, as in the case of pomegranate, but the fruit is sweet, and if one pours wine over it, they say it becomes sweeter and that it makes the wine sweeter' (IV.3.3). Pliny on the other hand claims that the Egyptians also ate the kernel (*NH*.XIII. xxxiii). Athenaeus, quoting a certain Agathocles of Cyzicus in the Propontis describes the tree, called by the Alexandrians 'konnaros' and 'paliuros'. He says that the fruit is very sweet and can be eaten while it is still green. When dried the Alexandrians grind it into meal, and this they eat without kneading and soaking in water, but simply in its natural condition. Athenaeus continues to say that he himself has often been served the fruit in Alexandria (*Deipnosophistes* XIV. 649–50).

Zizyphus appears to have been part of the pharaonic diet, and it naturally came to play a part in medicine. Almost all parts of the tree were used, even sawdust from the wood, which was otherwise used in carpentry.

A maceration of the leaves and a number of other ingredients were used to treat constipation in the right half of the belly (E 210), or with leaves of acacia and an unidentified ingredient they were mixed with 'carob(?) water' as an enema to 'cool the anus' (E 159). A cooling bandage for a finger or toe consisted of:

acacia leaves 1/4; zizyphus leaves 1/4; ochre 1/32; powdered malachite 1/32; the interior of a mussel 1/8; is ground and applied. (E 616)

A refreshing and tonic bandage was prepared to 'cool the vessels and strengthen weakness':

zizyphus leaves 1; acacia leaves 1; honey 1; is pounded in this honey and [the member] is bandaged with it for four days. (Ram v No. xii)

The fruits were sometimes made into bread. Two such loaves have actually been found. Apart from being eaten as part of the meal, they were also used in medicine:

treatment of anything from which a patient may suffer: zizyphus bread is boiled in water. Use it as a bandage when it is agreeably warm. (E 536)

A liver disease was treated with a mixture of zizyphus bread, figs, grapes, carob pod pulp(?), frankincense and three unidentified ingredients to be taken internally (E 480).

The Egyptian peasants at the beginning of the present century still used to make zizyphus bread. The fruits were placed in a wooden mortar and pounded to separate the flesh from the kernels. The flesh was reduced to powder and then shaken on a mat to clean it. After this it was kneaded with water to form a smooth dough and poured into dried gourds. A hole was dug in the ground and covered with leaves of the mudar plant (*Calotropis procera*). A fire was lit in the hole and the gourds left there in the warmth all night. The loaves were eaten on their own, or with clotted milk, in which case it had a constipatory effect.

The wood was blended with a liquid ingredient and used as an unguent for a male urinary disease (E 272). Zizyphus fruits were a component of an unguent with 'fruits' of sycamore and willow, and emmer grains ground to a mass with an unidentified ingredient and mixed with gum water. The resulting remedy was applied to any swollen member (E 582).

In the Coptic medical texts zizyphus fruits are mentioned just once in a treatment of the anus along with resin, myrrh and an unidentified ingredient. The remedy was to be taken 'with hot water in the bath' (Ch 225).

Identifying ancient Egyptian plants

The plants included in this book represent but a small selection of the ancient Egyptian flora, including only trees, herbs and flowers which can be identified with some degree of certainty. Any reservations have been pointed out in the text.

The identification of an ancient plant is no straightforward task, although for Egypt more information is available than in most extinct civilisations. Due to the fortunate climatic conditions and the Egyptian custom of placing a variety of items of daily life in their tombs, a fair number of actual plants have survived. Modern excavators are aware of the possibilities even a rubbish dump has to offer in that respect. If the remains of a plant can thus be identified with certainty, it is only possible to gauge its full use in Egypt if the plant's name can be established and found in textual sources, above all in the corpus of medical texts. These were compiled at an early date, that is to say before a host of new plants reached Egypt during the course of the New Kingdom, so the use of these arrivals in the Egyptian pharmacopoeia was not recorded. The ideal situation is to find a handful of seeds or berries in a pot with the name of the contents written on it, such as a jar of almonds from the tomb of Tutankhamun, and a pot of tiger nuts discovered in excavations at Aswân.

Among the ancient Egyptian sources are representations of plants, especially in scenes depicting gardens and the presentation of elaborate composite bouquets. The Egyptian artist had a particular attitude to his subject, be it a plant, a piece of furniture, a human being or any other motif. Realistic as his

A tree in a wall-painting in Theban Tomb no. 15; 18th Dynasty. The tree is unusual, if not unique. It bears some resemblance to a *Cassia fistula* L. as depicted in Prospero Alpini, *Plantes d'Égypte*, Ch. II.

efforts may appear, they are very often not at all so, and it is only through habit and frequent contact with Egyptian art that the artist's mode of representation is taken for granted. This has been pointed out with regard to the way in which he dealt with representations of the human figure, and in his interpretation of perspective. His concept of floral motifs was basically similar: it is the *idea* of a plant or a tree that is represented, not an illustration to a botanical handbook. Hence an identification of a plant on purely botanical grounds is often unsatisfactory.

It is a well-known fact that with few exceptions in ancient Egyptian art a tree is a tree, and there is little or no attempt at distinguishing, for instance, a rare incense tree from a common acacia. When fruits or pods are added, we can tell the difference between a fig and an acacia (which could on the other hand be a carob and not an acacia). Representations from the Old Kingdom of grape vines are indistinguishable from pictures of melons or cucumbers, unless the plant is provided with a support, suggesting a vine, or the fruit is marked with circles, indicating the individual grapes. A persea fruit as drawn by the ancient artist has the same outline and colour as the mandrake fruit. What appears to be a chrysanthemum may be a camomile or perhaps another composite flower, and the identification of the bright red poppy has still not been unanimously accepted. But nowhere are opinions more divided than when it comes to the climbing or trailing plant most frequently called 'convolvulus'. The plant appears to be depicted in varying forms, so that, given the Egyptians' attitude towards representation and the tendency for a motif to become stylised over the centuries, it is still not established beyond doubt whether the same plant is portrayed in each case. It may be that the variations are less significant in themselves than the different contexts in which they are shown. Perhaps in the end the variants are one and the same plant which incorporates a number of ideas, making it the 'ideal plant' for some purpose – and totally confusing the issue for the modern researcher.

The most characteristic feature of the plant in question is its dark-green triangular leaves, at times three-lobed or even five-lobed, or with serrated edges. The three-lobed leaves are shown in countless scenes, particularly of Ramesside date. It is this plant which frames scenes in the birth chamber so frequently depicted on ostraca; it is also seen in representations of an erotic nature, enveloping a naked musician or entwined around a chariot in an even more explicitly erotic scene, and, on a formal occasion, decorating the bed on which one of Akhenaten's daughters lies, having apparently died in childbirth. It is also found on women's coffins. The simple triangular shape can be found on plants climbing up papyrus stems in formal bouquets, but occasionally the leaves are rounded rather than triangular. The five-lobed and serrated variety decorates offering tables of late Ramesside date.

The plant(s) in question has a pliable stem. It may climb up or hang down. Occasionally we find a group of green dots which could represent berries or a cluster of tiny flowers, but no other flowers appear to be depicted. The lobed leaves and the berries have led some to identify the plant as ivy. However, there is no other evidence in the form of plant remains of ivy in pharaonic Egypt, and the climate is not really damp enough for the plant to feel at home there. The triangular leaves, and some of the three-lobed ones, would suggest convolvulus, especially in view of the prolific climbing habit of this plant. But then the 'berries' present a problem, and why were the flowers not shown?

It is possible to suggest alternative candidates, based on the appearance of the plant alone: black bryony (*Tamus communis* L.), a perennial with twining stem, dark glossy broadly ovate leaves with very long petioles, and small yellowish-green flowers followed by red berries. The plant is thought to be the 'wild *ampelos*' of Dioscorides (IV.183). The commentaries of Theophrastus (IX.20.3), on the other hand, suggest that his 'wild *ampelos*' was *Bryonia cretica*. A member of *bryonia*, *Bryonia dioica*, or white bryony, still grows in Egypt (as does

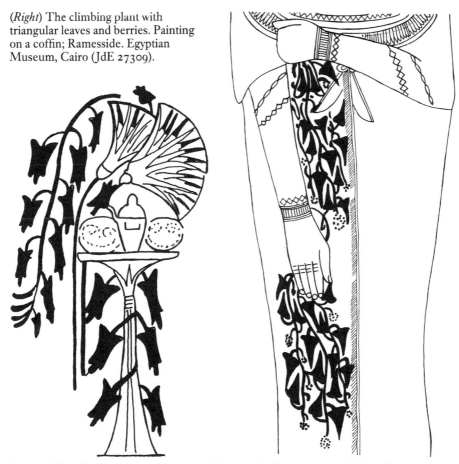

(*Right*) The climbing plant with triangular leaves and berries. Painting on a coffin; Ramesside. Egyptian Museum, Cairo (JdE 27309).

(*Above*) The climbing plant with 5-lobed leaves. Wall-painting in Theban Tomb no. 113 (now destroyed), after a drawing by Hay; Ramesside. British Library (Hay MSS 29822, 117).

Bryonia cretica). For this plant see in the Herbal. *Smilax* may also come into question. This is a woody vine climbing by means of tendrils, with prickly stems and alternate variable leaves, and white or greenish flowers followed by berries. Dioscorides mentions a plant whose Egyptian name was *lyiathe* (IV.144). This has been interpreted as *Smilax aspera*. It was made into a beverage for newborn babies and was believed to ward off snakes. According to Theophrastus (III.18.11–13) the berries were similar to those of bryony, hanging down like a grape cluster. Pliny says that the plant resembled the ivy. In his days it had a 'mournful' association (*NH*.XVI.lxiii cf. XXI.xxviii).

The ideas of babies and snakes are brought together in another plant which to the present writer is the most likely candidate: *Aristolochia serpentaria* L. (snakeroot) and *Aristolochia clematitis* L. (birthwort) (see the entry in the Herbal). Beliefs and practices among ancient people were long-lived, and it is worth considering the possibility that the connection between the plant depicted by the Egyptians and the world of women was maintained from remote antiquity until more recent times.

A more laborious approach to determining a plant quoted in the texts is to study its use in medicine and compare the ancient records with modern herbal medicine, or the use of the plant in other ancient civilisations. The classical authors are an inexhaustible source of information on these matters, and the task is greatly facilitated when one of these latter authorities actually makes reference to herbs grown, or at least used, in Egypt, be it in medicine or in cooking.

The linguist would attempt to compare ancient Egyptian words designating plants, or parts of plants, with terms used by the Copts. Useful comparisons can be made with plants mentioned in Sumerian, Babylonian, Assyrian and Biblical sources. One of the most intriguing compilations of Egyptian plant names can be made from the works of Dioscorides, who wrote in Greek but whose editors often quoted foreign plant names, including Egyptian ones. This list could be compared with the enumeration of more than 150 unidentified plant items listed by Renate Germer in her study of medicinal plants (*Arzneimittelpflanzen*; see Bibliography). A study of the two lists of names would appear to provide a golden opportunity for a linguist with botanical interests.

The Egyptian plant names quoted by Dioscorides

Frequent mention has been made of Dioscorides and his Egyptian plant names. These were not actually given by Dioscorides himself, but were added about a hundred years later in the second century AD. The mere fact that the Egyptians were alleged to possess a vocabulary of the more than one hundred herbs quoted suggests that the plants were known to them, although some of them were probably not native to Egypt.

The list of names is given below in full to offer a glimpse of the variety of plants available to the ancient herbalist. The Latin names are those given in the edition by Gunther, which is in turn based on the seventeenth-century translation by Goodyer (see Bibliography). The references to Dioscorides are also to the edition by Gunther, but additional references are given (in brackets) to an edition of the original Greek text by M. Wellmann, *Pedanii Dioscuridis Anarzarbei de Materia medica libri V* (Berlin 1906–14). The paragraphs in the two editions, based on different manuscripts, do not always correspond, and the transliteration of the plant names in Goodyer's hand shows variations from the Greek. The items marked with an asterisk are those dealt with in the present work.

Although some of the Egyptian names appear to be rather fanciful and un-Egyptian (as some of them probably were), others can be traced back to the ancient name, as for example 'mekhmoutim' to *mḥmḥ* (purslane); 'semeth' to *smt* (cress); 'mit' to *m3tt* (celery); 'somi' to *sʿm* (wormwood); 'soum' to *sʿ3m* (chaste tree); 'sampsouchos' to *sm Sbk* ('herb of Sobk').

LATIN	ENGLISH	EGYPTIAN	DIOSCORIDES	
Lavandula stoechas	Lavender	*suphlo*	III.31	(III.26)
Lepidum sativum	Cress	*semeth*	II.185	(II.155)
Lilium candidum	Lily	*larsaora, ombrisedo, somphaiphou, tialos*	III.116	(III.102)
Lilium chalcedonicum	—	*iokry*	III.137	(III.122)
Lupinus pilosus (?)	Lupin	*brekhou*	II.132	(II.109)
Lychnis coronaria	Rose campion	*semeom*	III.114	
Malva sylvestris	Hollyhock	*khokorten*	II.144	(II.118)
Mandragora officinarum	Mandrake	*aperioum*	II.76	(II.75)
Marrubium vulgare	White horehound	*asterispa*	III.119	(III.105)
Melilotus	Sweet clover	*aimeith*	III.48	(III.40)
Mentha sativa	Mint	*makitho, perxo, pherthroumonthou, tis*	III.41	(III.34)
Mentha torgifolia	Curled mint	*bellou, thesmouzoei*	III.43	(III.35)
Mercurialis annua	French mercury	*aphlopho*	IV.191	(IV.189)
Micropus erectus	—	*daphnoines*	IV.131	(IV.133)
Nerium oleander	Oleander	*skhinphi*	IV.82	(IV.81)
Opopanax hispidus(?)	—	*napo*	III.55	(III.48)
Origanum majorana	Marjoram	*sopho*	III.47	(III.39)
Papaver rhoeas, P. somniferum	Poppy	*nanti*	IV.64	(IV.63)
Pastinaca graeca	Greek parsnip	*khemis*	III.80	(III.69)
Petroselinum sativum	Parsley	*anonim*	III.76	(III.65)
Pimpinella dissecta	—	*erxoen*	IV.124	(IV.123)
Plantago major, P. lagopus	Greater plantain	*asoeth*	II.153	(II.126)
Polygonum aviculare	Knotgrass	*thephin*	IV.4	(IV.4)
Portulaca oleracea	Purslane	*mokhmoutim*	II.151	(II.124)
Potamogeton	Pondweed	*ethegkhis, loikhor*	IV.101	(IV.100)
Potentilla reptans	Cinquefoil	*agophitebeoki*	IV.42	(IV.42)
Prangos ferulacea	—	*sampsoth*	III.82	(III.71)
Prenanthes purpurea	—	*ai*	III.87	(III.74)
Ranunculus acris	Buttercup	*methou*	II.206	(II.175)
Ricinus communis	Castor-oil plant	*sesthamna, trixin*	IV.164	(IV.161)
Rubia tinctorum	Madder	*sophobi*	III.160	(III.143)
Rubus fruticosus, R. ulmifolius	Bramble	*aimoios, ametros*	IV.37	(IV.37)

LATIN	ENGLISH	EGYPTIAN	DIOSCORIDES	
Rumex patientia	Dock	*semith*	II.140	(II.114)
Ruta graveolens	Rue	*ephnoubon*	III.52	(III.45)
Salvia officinalis	Sage	*apousi*	III.40	(III.33)
Santolina maritima	—	*semeon*	III.132	(III.117)
Saponaria officinalis	Soapwort	*oino*	II.193	(II.163)
Satureia thymbra(?)	Savory	*sekemmene*	III.45	(III.37)
Scolymus hispanicus	Garden thistle	*knous*	III.16	(III.14)
Scrophularia peregrina	Nettle-leaved figwort	*aithopi*	IV.93	(IV.94)
Sedum ochroleucum	Stonecrop	*etieikelta*	IV.90	(IV.89)
Sempervivum arboreum	Houseleek	*pamphanes*	IV.89	(IV.88)
Sideritis remota	Ironwort	*senodionor*	IV.33	(IV.33)
Sinapis arvensis	Mustard	*euthmoi*	II.142	(II.116)
Sisymbrium officinale	Hedge mustard	*erethmou*	II.188	(II.158)
Smilax aspera	Sarsaparilla	*lyiathe*	IV.144	(IV.142)
Solanum nigrum	Garden nightshade	*alelo*	IV.71	(IV.70)
Stratiotes aloides	Water soldier	*tibour*	IV.102	(IV.101)
Teucrium scordioides	Water germander	*aphon*	II.125	(III.111)
Thlaspi bursa pastoris	Shepherd's purse	*souitempsou*	II.186	(II.156)
Thymus capitata	Cretan thyme	*stephanoi*	III.44	(III.36)
Thymus spicata	—	*saem*	III.30	(III.25)
Thymus sibthorpii	Thyme	*merouopyos*	III.46	(III.38)
Tragium columnae	—	*sober*	IV.50	(IV.49)
Trigonella foenum-graecum	Fenugreek	*itasin*	II.124	(II.102)
Tussilago farfara	Coltsfoot	*saarthra*	III.126	(III.112)
Urtica pilulifera, U. urens	Roman nettle, small nettle	*selepsiou*	IV.94	(IV.93)
Veratrum album	White hellebore	*somphis, ounre*	IV.150	(IV.148)
Verbascum sp.	Mullein	*athal*	IV.104	(IV.103)
Verbena officinalis	Vervain	*pempsempte*	IV.60	(IV.59)
Verbena supina	—	*pemphemphtham*	IV.61	(IV.60)
Vinca minor	Lesser periwinkle	*philakouon*	IV.7	(III.180)
Vitex agnus-castus	Chaste tree	*soum*	I.135	(I.103)

Glossary of terms

analgesic	relieving pain
antihelmintic	destroying intestinal worms
antiseptic	counteracting infection
callosity	thickness of skin
carminative	relieving flatulence
demulcent	soothing
diaphoretic	increasing perspiration
diuretic	stimulating the flow of urine
emetic	causing vomiting
emmenagogue	stimulating menstrual flow
emollient	softening
euphoric	provoking a feeling of well-being
expectorant	promoting expulsion of fluid from the lungs
flatulence	condition caused by gas accumulating in the stomach
hydragogue	expelling water
latex	milky fluid of plant
laxative	loosening the bowels
narcotic	inducing sleep, stupefaction or death
purgative	powerful laxative
sedative	soothing medicine which calms the nerves
stimulant	increasing energy
stomachich	relieving cramps
vermifuge	expelling intestinal worms

Chronological Table

Old Kingdom	3rd–6th Dynasties		*c.*2686–*c.*2181 BC
Middle Kingdom	11th Dynasty	Mentuhotpe I–III	2133–1991 BC
	12th Dynasty	Sesostris I–III Amenemhet I–IV	1991–1786 BC
New Kingdom	18th Dynasty	Tuthmosis I–IV Amenophis I–IV Tutankhamun	1567–1320 BC
	19th Dynasty	Ramesses I–II Sethos I–II	1320–1200 BC
	20th Dynasty	Ramesses III–XI	1200–1085 BC
Late Period	21st–30th Dynasties		1035–332 BC
Ptolemaic Period			332–31 BC
Roman Period			31 BC–AD 395

Bibliography

The ancient Egyptian medical texts are transcribed, translated and discussed in H. von Deines, H. Grapow and W. Westendorf, *Grundriss der Medizin der alten Ägypter*, 9 vols, Berlin 1954–73. The Coptic medical texts are translated and discussed in W. C. Till, *Die Arzneikunde der Kopten*, Berlin 1951.

Major works including a discussion of ancient Egyptian herbs

CHARPENTIER, G. *Recueil de matériaux épigraphiques relatifs à la botanique de l'Égypte antique*, Paris 1981

DARBY, W. J. GHALIOUNGUI, P. and GRIVETTI, L. *Food: The Gift of Osiris* I–II, London/New York/San Francisco 1977

GERMER, R. *Flora des pharaonischen Ägypten*, Mainz 1985

GERMER, R. *Untersuchung über Arzneimittelpflanzen im alten Ägypten*, Hamburg 1979

GERMER, R. *Die Pflanzenmaterialien aus dem Grab des Tutankhamun*, Hildesheim 1989.

HEPPER, F. Nigel, *Pharaoh's Flowers. The Botanical Treasures of Tutankhamun*, London 1990.

KEIMER, L. *Die Gartenpflanzen im alten Ägypten*, I Berlin 1924 (repr. Hildesheim 1967); II (ed. R. Germer), Mainz am Rhein 1984

LORET, V. 'Le Kyphie', *Journal Asiatique*, 8e série, x, 1857, pp.76–132

LUCAS, A. *Ancient Egyptian Materials and Industries*, 4th edn, revised by J. R. Harris, London 1962. This work includes chapters on cosmetics and perfume.

Egypt's Golden Age: The Art of Living in the New Kingdom 1558–1085 B.C., exhibition catalogue, Museum of Fine Arts, Boston 1982, with chapters on The Garden, Food and Drink, Toilette Implements, Cosmetic Arts and Medicine.

Classical sources

APICIUS *The Roman Cookery Book* translated by B. Flower and E. Rosenbaum. London 1980

ATHENAEUS *The Deipnosophists* translated by C. B. Gulick. Loeb Classical Library 1959

DIODORUS *Diodorus of Sicily* translated by C. H. Oldfather. Loeb Classical Library 1968

DIOSCORIDES *The Greek Herbal of Dioscorides* translated by J. Goodyer (1655), edited by R. T. Gunther, Oxford 1934 (repr. New York 1959). Cf. also M. M. Sadek, *The Arabic Materia Medica of Dioscorides*, Quebec 1983

HERODOTUS *Herodotus I–II* translated by A. D. Godley. Loeb Classical Library 1946. Cf. also A. B. Lloyd, *Herodotus Book II. Commentary 1–98*, Leiden 1976

STRABO *The Geography of Strabo VIII* translated by H. L. Jones. Loeb Classical Library 1959

THEOPHRASTUS *Theophrastus. Enquiry into Plants and Minor Works on Odours and Weather Signs* translated by Sir Arthur Hort. Loeb Classical Library 1980

Other works on plants in antiquity

Bulletin on Sumerian Agriculture I– (Cambridge 1984–)

CAMPBELL THOMPSON, R. *A Dictionary of Assyrian Botany*, London 1949

CAMPBELL THOMPSON, R. *The Assyrian Herbal*, London 1924

DIMBLEBY, G. *Plants and Archaeology*, 2nd edn, London 1978

Löw, I. *Die Flora der Juden*, 4 vols, Wien 1924–34 (repr. 1967)

ZOHARY, M. *Plants of the Bible*, Cambridge 1982

Books on herbs and spices in modern times

ALPIN, P. *La Médicine des Égyptiens* I–II, Cairo 1980

ALPIN, P. *Plantes d'Égypte*, Cairo 1980

BEDEVIAN, A. K. *Illustrated Polyglottic Dictionary of Plant Names*, Cairo 1936

DUCROS, M. A. H. *Essai sur le droguier populaire arabe de l'inspectorat des pharmacies du Caire, Mémoires de l'Institut d'Égypte XI*, Cairo 1930

GARLAND, S. *The Herb and Spice Book*, London 1979

MORTON, J. F. *Major Medicinal Plants. Botany, Culture and Uses*, Springfield, Illinois 1977

STUART, M. (ed.) *The Encyclopedia of Herbs and Herbalism*, London 1979

The Medicine of The Prophet (*al-tibb al-Nabawi*) translated by P. Johnstone (in press)

Photographic acknowledgements

The author and publishers are grateful to the following for permission to reproduce the black and white photographs:

British Museum pp. 10, 39, 45
Griffith Institute, Ashmolean Museum, Oxford pp. 15, 28, 29 (*left*), 31, 35, 55, 122
A. Mekhitarian pp. 50, 53, 54 (photos courtesy of the Griffith Institute, Oxford)
Bokforlaget Natur och Kultur, Stockholm (reproduced from V. Täckholm, *Faraos Blomster*) pp. 77, 84, 104

The drawing on p. 29 (*right*) was by G. Schweinfurth; all other line drawings are copyright of Lise Manniche.

Index

General

Ailments and remedies

Plants

Entries in the Herbal are indicated by page numbers in **bold** type.